HTML5 Multimedia: Develop and Design

Ian Devlin

Peachpit Press

1249 Eighth Street
Berkeley, CA 94710
510/524-2178
510/524-2221 (fax)

Find us on the Web at: www.peachpit.com
To report errors, please send a note to: errata@peachpit.com
Peachpit Press is a division of Pearson Education.
Copyright © 2012 by Ian Devlin

Editor: Rebecca Gulick
Development and Copy Editor: Anne Marie Walker
Technical Reviewer: Chris Mills
Production Coordinator: Myrna Vladic
Compositor: David Van Ness
Proofreader: Patricia Pane
Indexer: Valerie Haynes-Perry
Cover Design: Aren Howell Straiger
Cover Production: Jaime Brenner
Interior Design: Mimi Heft

ISBN-13:   978-0-321-79393-5
ISBN-10:   0-321-79393-5

9 8 7 6 5 4 3 2 1

Printed and bound in the United States of America

Dedicated to the memory of Paul Fallon

Tá daoine a shiúlann inár saolta agus shiúlann amach astu go luath
Tá daoine a fhanann ar feadh tamaill
Agus fágann said rianta a gcos ar ár gcroíthe
Agus casann ár n-anamacha port nua go deo deo

ACKNOWLEDGMENTS

Writing a book is a time-consuming and difficult process, and one I knew nothing about before embarking on this project. A number of people have helped me through the book-writing process, and others have helped me through the HTML5 process, whether they know it or not. All deserve my thanks.

To Rebecca Gulick for giving me the opportunity to actually write this book and for clearly explaining to me the steps involved.

To Anne Marie Walker for ensuring that my words are clear and understandable.

To Chris Mills for his editing and technical reviewing skills, and providing me with many good suggestions and alterations throughout the text.

To Rich Clark for giving me the opportunity to curate for HTML5 Gallery (www.html5gallery.com), which not only increased my interest in and knowledge of HTML5, but it also led to me writing this book.

To Remy Sharp for first drawing my attention to HTML5 in an article in *.net* magazine back in October 2009.

To you, the reader, for deciding to purchase this book with the intention of learning. I hope you find it enjoyable and educational.

CONTENTS

INTRODUCTION

As a web developer or web designer, or those of you who just maintain your own website, you know that the web is constantly changing, and the tools and methods that are used to build websites are in constant development. Like sand dunes in the Sahara, they shift constantly, but fortunately, usually in a forward direction.

The shift in web technologies has currently arrived at HTML5, the latest version of the language used to define and build web pages. With it comes an easier method of adding multimedia to your web pages.

The goal of this book is to provide you with an introduction to adding audio and video to your website, and to give you a glimpse of what else you can do with HTML5 multimedia.

Throughout the book you'll find in-depth details of the various HTML5 multimedia elements, as well as full code examples on how you can use them to add audio and video to your website. You'll also learn about the accompanying JavaScript API that allows you to create your own media controls.

In addition, you'll find explanations and examples of how you can style the HTML5 media elements with CSS, including some of the new features that CSS3 has to offer. You'll also learn about multimedia and accessibility, and how you can add subtitles to your website video.

WHO THIS BOOK IS FOR

This book is aimed at those who are starting out with HTML5 and adding HTML5 audio and video to their websites, and those who are already familiar with HTML5 multimedia but want to learn more.

Some basic knowledge of HTML and CSS is assumed, and the later chapters require at least a rudimentary knowledge of JavaScript. That said, all the examples on the book's accompanying website at www.html5multimedia.com are complete.

SCREEN SHOTS AND BROWSER VERSIONS

During the course of writing this book, some browser vendors released newer versions of their products. Firefox is now on version 7, Chrome is on version 14, and Safari has moved to 5.1. The screen shots in the book usually indicate which browser and version it was taken from at the time the chapter was written. This, of course, means that some of the screen shots are from older versions of the browser. But rest assured that they still work just as well in the latest versions, and if they don't, it is clearly marked.

THE WEBSITE FOR THIS BOOK

All the code used in the examples in this book is on the accompanying website at www.html5multimedia.com. You can either download the files in their entirety or navigate to the various files via the website and see them working online.

CONTACT

If you would like to contact me, you can do so at info@html5multimedia.com.

BEFORE YOU BEGIN

In the later chapters of this book, some of what you'll read is experimental due to specifications that were still in development at the time of this writing and poor or nonexistent support in browsers. This of course may have changed by the time you have this book in your hands. The book's website will indicate improved support where applicable.

It's time to begin! Let's start by taking a quick look at HTML5, what it is, and where it comes from.

1

AN **INTRODUCTION** TO **HTML5**

HTML5 is a major overhaul of the language that nearly all the content on the Internet is effectively displayed in. Indeed, HTML5 changes the way you think about the HTML markup language. As well as introducing new markup elements to the specification, a host of JavaScript APIs are also included to give developers a deeper and consistent way to access native functionality across browsers. Designers and those who are "not too techy" will also benefit. They'll now be able to carry out complex tasks and easily add multimedia to a web document that in the past would have required more technical knowledge.

This chapter provides you with a brief introduction to HTML5 and how it came about. You'll also take a quick look at some of the main HTML5 structural elements.

Let's go forth and learn!

WHAT IS HTML5?

HTML5 is the latest and greatest version of the core language of the World Wide Web and is one of the most exciting developments to happen to the web and the web community in a long time. HTML (HyperText Markup Language) is the language that has been at the heart of all web documents since its conception in the early 1990s.

HTML5's predecessor is HTML 4.01, and one of the major differences between HTML 4.01 and HTML5 is the addition of many JavaScript APIs (Application Programming Interfaces) to the specification. Of course, one of these specifications is directly relevant to the subject of this book—the API that allows interactions with multimedia elements within the browser. As well as these new APIs, HTML5 also alters the meaning of some existing HTML elements, removes others, and more important, adds new ones—some of which allow you to provide more semantic meaning to your content.

It's worthwhile noting that most of these new elements don't actually add any new functionality that you've not seen before.

But before you dive into the workings of HTML5, let's first look at where HTML5 came from and how it evolved.

THE PROGRESSION OF HTML5

It's fairly common knowledge that Tim Berners-Lee is the father of HTML and what everyone recognises as the web today.

There is no need to go into a long and detailed history of HTML's growth from the initial version in 1990 to the version that most of you will have been brought up on, HTML 4.01. But it is worthwhile looking at how HTML5 came into fruition and then evolved.

In 1998, the members of the World Wide Web Consortium (W3C; www.w3.org) decided that it wouldn't be worth their while to extend the HTML specification beyond HTML 4.01. They decided that the future of the web lay with XML (eXtensible Markup Language) due to its stricter syntax, which also made the processing of XML web documents much easier.

Laying HTML 4.01 to rest, they began working on a new specification for XHTML 1.0, which basically was a reformulation of HTML 4.01 as an XML vocabulary that contained several strict syntax rules. Personally, I was quite a fan of this, because I liked the uniformity of it all, but not everyone was convinced. So, two flavours of XHTML were created: XHTML Transitional to help convert the non-believers and XHTML Strict, which was for the true believers and what (the W3C hoped) the nonbelievers would eventually strive to follow.

The situation remained like this for a number of years, with the nonbelievers either reverting back to HTML 4.01 or remaining satisfied with XHTML Transitional. As the W3C's dream of a stricter XHTML world began to dissipate, its members soldiered on and began working on the specification for XHTML 2.0.

This seemed a bit of an odd decision, because XHTML wasn't as widely supported as the W3C hoped. Internet Explorer (IE), one of the most widespread browsers at the time (it still is, just less so), didn't even support XHTML. In fact, declaring a web document as XHTML would only cause IE to attempt to download the page and not even render it! In addition, forging ahead with a new specification in XHTML 2.0 didn't reflect what web developers in the real world were actually doing at the time. Also, it wasn't backwards compatible, which, as you will learn later, is another of HTML5's strengths.

HTML5 AND **BACKWARDS COMPATIBILITY**

One of the first HTML documents ever written, "Links and Anchors," (www.w3.org/History/19921103-hypertext/hypertext/WWW/Link.html) is almost valid HTML5!

In February 2004, a separate group—which included people from Opera, Mozilla, and later, Apple—called the WHATWG (Web Hypertext Application Technology Group; www.whatwg.org) released a draft of a new specification—Web Forms 2.0—that aimed to extend HTML forms. This specification had no standing with the W3C, and in fact the specification states:

"This document currently has no official standing within the W3C at all. It is the result of loose collaboration between interested parties over dinner, in various mailing lists, on IRC, and in private e-mail."

The state of affairs continued this way with the W3C pursuing XHTML 2.0 and the WHATWG taking its own path, which included beginning work on another specification, Web Applications 1.0. As it turns out, Web Applications 1.0 was the precursor to what is now known as HTML5.

The situation took a turn for the better in 2006 when the W3C had a change of heart with regards to XHTML and decided to no longer pursue it. In 2007, the Fifth W3C HTML Working Group was chartered, and the W3C also announced that it would allow the charter for the XHTML 2 Working Group to expire at the end of 2009. Using the WHATWG's Web Applications specification as a base, both the W3C and the WHATWG began developing a new HTML specification, although somewhat bizarrely, it wasn't a collaborative process.

As a result, there are actually two different versions of the specification, although the editor of both is Ian Hickson of Google. Fortunately, there aren't many differences between the two; the main difference is how they are maintained. The WHATWG specification is a "continuously maintained living standard"; it is maintained on a section-by-section granular scale. The W3C specification on the other hand follows the more traditional style of staged releases. Content-wise they're largely the same, although one of the main differences (at time of this writing) is that the WHATWG version includes the WebVTT file format and some text-track API features (which are discussed in Chapter 8) that the W3C version does not.

Currently, both the W3C and WHATWG versions of the HTML5 specification are in a stage called "Last Call," which means internal and external communities to the W3C are invited to confirm the technical soundness of the specification.

HTML5 SPECIFICATIONS

Two different versions of the HTML5 specification are available at this time, but there are a few other versions that are also worth taking a look at:

- **W3C HTML5 Specification.** The latest published version is at www.w3.org/TR/html5. This version is what is closest to being final.

- **WHATWG HTML5 Specification.** The latest living standard is at www.whatwg.org/specs/web-apps/current-work/multipage. Generally, newer additions get added to this specification first, before finally making it to the W3C specification.

- **WHATWG HTML5 Specification—Edition for Web Developers.** The web developer edition is at http://developers.whatwg.org. This is a nice, easy-to-look at version of the WHATWG specification that is usually kept in sync with the living standard but can be out of date.

WHEN CAN YOU USE HTML5?

Actually, you can use HTML5 now. Many existing websites are written in HTML5, of which you are probably already aware. Although the current target date for the HTML5 specification to reach recommendation status is 2014, this does not mean you cannot use it.

At the time of this writing, all the latest versions of the main browsers support some, if not most, features of HTML5. Even IE9 finally supports HTML5 markup and functionality. This should help to remove any misgivings you might have with regards to browser compatibility.

You shouldn't be worried that the HTML5 specification won't reach recommendation status for another few years. To put this into perspective, the specification for CSS2.1 only reached recommendation status on the 7th of June, 2011. And CSS3 is all the rage at the moment.

With this in mind, let's move on and take a look at some of the new structural elements of HTML5.

MAIN **HTML5**
STRUCTURAL ELEMENTS

Any use of the HTML5 multimedia elements and APIs that this book discusses will naturally require writing HTML markup. You could of course use HTML 4.01 markup (although you do need to use the HTML5 DOCTYPE mentioned in this section), but because this book is about HTML5 multimedia, it makes sense for you to use HTML5 markup. All the examples throughout this book and on the website use HTML5 markup.

Let's start by taking a quick look at the main structural elements that can make up an HTML5 document.

DOCTYPE AND CHARSET

As with any HTML document, you need to begin an HTML5 document with a DOCTYPE. A DOCTYPE tells the browser what version of HTML the page in question uses, and the browser in turn uses this to determine how to render the page. The great thing about the HTML5 DOCTYPE is its simplicity.

With HTML 4.01, you might write this:

```
<!DOCTYPE HTML PUBLIC "-//W3C//DTD HTML 4.01//EN"
"http://www.w3.org/TR/html4/strict.dtd">
```

But in HTML5, you'd write this:

```
<!DOCTYPE html>
```

Yep. That's it. Nothing more.

This new DOCTYPE is the shortest valid string that will cause the browser to render the document in standards mode, which you want, rather than quirks mode, which you definitely don't want (see the sidebar "Standards Mode vs. Quirks Mode" for more details).

STANDARDS MODE VS. QUIRKS MODE

Modern browsers can use two different modes to interpret the CSS of a web document: standards mode and quirks mode.

Standards mode causes the browser to render the CSS according to the specification, which is correct and the way you would want it.

Quirks mode on the other hand causes the browser to render the CSS according to old, nonspecification rules. This mode exists for backwards compatibility because older browsers didn't render CSS according to the specifications.

These days standards mode is the one you want to use, because in most cases the oldest browser you will be supporting will be IE6, which doesn't need quirks mode to work correctly (although it probably will require some IE6 specific CSS, but chances are you already know that!).

Interestingly, or annoyingly, IE versions 6 to 8 render a web document as IE5.5 would when they render a quirks mode page. And you definitely don't want this because the resulting rendered page is unpredictable!

It's also useful and a good idea to provide the character encoding of the document, which is usually UTF-8. Specifying this in your markup has also been highly simplified in HTML5.

In HTML 4.01, the charset would be set via this line:

```
<meta http-equiv="Content-Type" content="text/html; charset=UTF-8">
```

In HTML5, you'd use:

```
<meta charset="utf-8">
```

As with the DOCTYPE, this character encoding string contains the minimum number of characters required to be interpreted by the web browser. In fact, you could make it two characters shorter by removing the quotes, but my personal choice is to include them here. Also, I've not closed the element, which again I don't have to, but I could if I wanted to. HTML5 isn't that strict.

TIP: Specifying a charset also prevents a cross-site scripting vulnerability issue in IE7.

NAMING THE NEW HTML5 ELEMENTS

Some of the new elements that came to be included in the HTML5 specification weren't just randomly chosen.

In 2004, the editor of the HTML5 specification, Google's Ian Hickson, carried out a data-mining experiment using the Google index on over 1 billion web pages to get a better idea of what the web was actually made of with regards to web document content. He published a number of analyses, one of which identifies the most popular CSS class names used for HTML elements. You can read this analysis at http://code.google.com/webstats/2005-12/classes.html. The top 10 CSS class names and their corresponding HTML5 elements are listed in **Table 1.1**.

Although Table 1.1 doesn't cover all of the new HTML5 elements that have been added, it does show you that there was some thought behind the naming of the new HTML5 elements and the semantic content they represent.

TABLE 1.1 Top 10 Most Popular HTML Class Names and Their Corresponding HTML5 Elements

RANK	NAME	HTML5 ELEMENT
1	footer	\<footer>
2	menu	\<menu>
3	title	\<header>
4	small	\<small>
5	text	\<article>, \<section>, \<aside>
6	content	\<article>, \<section>, \<aside>
7	header	\<header>
8	nav	\<nav>
9	copyright	n/a
10	button	n/a

<HEADER> AND <FOOTER>

Almost every HTML document has a header and footer. The HTML5 specification recognises this and includes two specific elements that you can use to semantically identify a header and footer. These elements are not restricted to one per document, however, and can be used to specify the header and footer areas of a particular section or article of a document.

The header element usually contains at least one h element:

```
<header>
    <h1>The header element</h1>
    <span class="subtitle">A quick guide</span>
</header>
```

The footer element is just as simple to use and requires no explanation:

```
<footer>
    <small>Copyright &copy; 2011</small>
</footer>
```

The header element doesn't have to appear at the top of the web document, just as the footer element doesn't have to be placed at the bottom. You can actually place either wherever you want to. That said, it often makes sense to do so, just so the source of the document is easier to read.

‹HGROUP›

If a header contains a number of h elements grouped together, they can be contained within an hgroup element like this:

```
<header>
    <hgroup>
        <h1>The header element</h1>
        <h2>A quick guide</h2>
    </hgroup>
    <a href="home.html">Home</a>
</header>
```

Note that the hgroup element can *only* contain h elements and nothing else.

HGROUP **CONTROVERSY!**

The hgroup element is a bit controversial at the time of this writing, because it has been removed and reinserted into the HTML5 specification in the last few months. Efforts are being made to remove it again and possibly replace it with something more semantic. So by the time you read this, it might be omitted from the specification, so it's worth double-checking.

‹ARTICLE› AND ‹SECTION›

When you're laying out a web page with HTML, you often use the div element to indicate specific sections of your document. This usually works well and is all that is needed. But what if you wanted to give your section a particular semantic meaning so it's more than "just a div"?

This is where the article and section elements come in, and there's often a bit of confusion as to which one to use and when. The confusion arises because you're forced to think a bit more about what you're writing and the way you present it.

If you simply want to contain information for styling purposes only, the div element is the one to use. The reason is that the content within the div doesn't have any specific semantic meaning, for example, when using it as a "wrapper" element to help position some columns in the centre of a page:

```
<div class="wrapper">
    <div class="columnOne">This is column one</div>
    <div class="columnTwo">This is column two</div>
</div>
```

If you decide that the content actually does have a semantic meaning, you need to look closely at what that meaning is. The W3C HTML5 specification actually defines a section element as representing

> "a generic section of a document or application. A section, in this context, is a thematic grouping of content, typically with a heading."

So if the content you want to contain all fits nicely under the one heading, a section element is probably the way to go. But before you make the final decision on using a section element, let's take a quick look at the article element, which is a specific type of section element. Once again, the W3C specification encourages you to use the article element

> "when it would make sense to syndicate the contents of the element."

But what does this mean, exactly?

Well, as an example, think about the layout of a newspaper article. A newspaper article might contain several sections, each of which has its own heading. But overall, the sections relate to each other and fit together, because they talk about the same story. If this is the case in your content, the `article` element is the one to use.

But bear in mind that the `article` element doesn't relate to the idea of a newspaper article, just the way it is laid out. An `article` can also represent an article of clothing in your wardrobe, because it's a generic term that refers to a single unit of content that stands alone and can be syndicated. But it can also relate to other articles that it sits beside.

Of course, the newspaper article analogy also shows that you can nest `section` elements within `article` elements and vice versa. But as with the `div` element, don't make the content too muddled or have too much nesting!

Putting the `article` and `section` elements together, your content might look something like this:

```
<article>
    <header>
        <h1>HTML5 Multimedia</h1>
        <span class="subtitle">The way forward!</span>
    </header>
    <section>
        <header>
            <h2>Video</h2>
        </header>
        <p>This section talks about video...</p>
    </section>
    <section>
        <header>
            <h2>Audio</h2>
        </header>
        <p>This section talks about audio...</p>
    </section>
    <footer>
```

```
            <small>Written by Ian Devlin 2011</small>
        </footer>
    </article>
```

Using the preceding example, you can see how the idea of using the `article` and `section` elements within your content can be put into practice. The example has two sections, one contains information about video and the other contains information about audio. They are clearly separate from each other and therefore should be contained within separate `section` elements.

Overall, however, they are related, coming together under the HTML5 Multimedia heading. So collectively they should go together under the same heading, either in an enclosing `section` or `article`. In this case, it does seem to make sense that the content could be syndicated (e.g., contained as an item in an RSS feed), so the `article` element seems most suitable.

Alternatively, as mentioned previously, you can have a number of `section` elements contained within an `article`, for example, on a news summary page that contains links to separate articles:

```
<section>
    <header>
        <h1>HTML5 News</h1>
    </header>
    <article>
        <header>
            <h2>HTML5 Multimedia</h2>
        </header>
        <p>In this article you will learn all about HTML5
        ⤷  Multimedia.</p>
        <a href="html5-multimedia.html">Read more...</a>
    </article>
    <article>
        <header>
```

```
            <h2>HTML5 and Semantic Structure</h2>
        </header>
        <p>This article is all about HTML5 and structural
    →   semantics.</p>
        <a href="html5-structural-semantics.html">Read more...</a>
    </article>
    <footer>
        <a href="news-list.html">View all</a>
    </footer>
</section>
```

As the examples also illustrate, the article and section elements can also contain header and footer elements if they make semantic sense, as they do here.

H ELEMENTS IN HTML5

A hot topic of discussion at the moment in the HTML5 world is that of h elements in the header element and whether multiple h1 elements should be used throughout a single document.

As you may have noticed in the examples in the "<article> and <section>" section, an h1 element has been used in the main header (be it in the overall article or section) and h2 elements in the sub section/article header elements. This was done for backwards compatibility purposes due to poor browser support (Firefox 5 and Chrome 12 excepted) for what is known as the *HTML5 Outlining Algorithm*.

The HTML5 Outlining Algorithm is defined as part of the HTML5 specification and is used to determine the structure of an HTML5 document using its headings, titles, and so on to map out the document. You can read about HTML5 Document Outlines at http://html5doctor.com/document-outlines.

At the moment it's advisable to stick to using the different h elements to maintain compatibility with older browsers. Naturally, support for the algorithm will improve with further browser releases, but as with everything, the decision is ultimately yours.

<NAV>

The nav element is used to contain the primary navigation throughout your site. So any links to separate pages, such as About, News, and your blog, can be included here.

It can also contain any links that are external to your site—that is, that take the user away from your site—for example, links to Twitter or Facebook accounts, as long as they constitute the primary navigation of your site.

The markup is easy, and the nav element usually contains an unordered list, but of course can also simply contain a number of hyperlinks to the pages in question:

```
<nav>
    <ul>
        <li>
            <a href="index.html">Home</a>
        </li>
        <li>
            <a href="about.html">About</a>
        </li>
        <li>
            <a href="contact.html">Contact</a>
        </li>
    </ul>
</nav>
```

The nav element is often contained within a header, although it doesn't have to be. It can also be contained within a footer element, but only if it's the primary navigation of your website. Because footers these days often contain a set of secondary site navigation links, they should not be contained within a nav element. However, it's OK to have more than one nav element on the same page, should its use be warranted.

<ASIDE>

The aside element is used to contain page non-main content that is relevant to the main content it sits next to, but the main content makes perfect sense on its own without it. The content of the aside element can also make sense on its own, although it doesn't have to.

A current, real-world use of the aside element is for sidebars, which of course can contain anything from widgets and social media feeds to related links and images:

```
<aside>
    <header>
        <h1>Twitter feed</h1>
    </header>
    <ul>
        <li>#HTML5 is awesome! - 26th June 2011 @ 14:30</li>
        <li>Everyone should be using #HTML5 - 26th June 2011 @
14:22</li>
    </ul>
    <footer>
        <a href="http://twitter.com/iandevlin">follow me!</a>
    </footer>
</aside>
```

Note how the aside element can also contain header and footer elements if they are appropriate.

FIGURE 1.1 An image and caption displayed with the figure and figcaption elements.

Figure 1 - The HTML5 logo in all its glory!

<FIGURE> AND <FIGCAPTION>

Two new elements were introduced to allow relating a multimedia element (image, video, or audio) to a specific caption, which of course makes the content contained within these new elements more semantic (there's that word again!): the figure element and the figcaption element.

The figcaption element can only exist within a figure element, although it doesn't have to be there; obviously, not all content will have a caption:

```
<figure>
    <img src="images/html5-logo.gif" alt="The HTML5 logo " />
    <figcaption>
        <strong>Figure 1 - </strong>The HTML5 logo in all its glory!
    </figcaption>
</figure>
```

Normally, you'd style the figcaption contents to appear in small text above an image or at the bottom (**Figure 1.1**). But of course you don't have to and can generally do with it whatever you want!

INTERNET EXPLORER AND BROWSER COMPATIBILITY

At the time of this writing, the latest versions of all major browsers support several of the new HTML5 elements, especially those mentioned in this chapter. IE8 and earlier, however, do not. These new elements are completely unknown to these browsers, and therefore, the browsers won't render them at all.

All is not lost however.

You can easily add the html5shim script by Remy Sharp (http://code.google.com/p/html5shiv) to the top of your web document:

```
<!--[if lt IE 9]>
    <script src="//html5shim.googlecode.com/svn/trunk/html5.js"></script>
<![endif]-->
```

This script tells IE all about the new elements that it may come across when rendering the document, so it happily does so.

For these older browsers, you also need to add some default CSS styling to certain elements so that the browser knows to render them as block-level elements:

```
<!--[if lt IE 9]>
    <style>
        article, aside, figure, footer, header, hgroup, menu, nav, section {
            display:block;
        }
    </style>
<![endif]-->
```

If you intend to set the innerHTML of an element or use jQuery with HTML5 and older versions of IE, you need to add the innerShiv script (http://jdbartlett.com/innershiv) to your web document.

You'll need to download this JavaScript file and host it yourself, and then add it in the same way as you would add the innershim file mentioned previously:

```
<!--[if lt IE 9]>
    <script src="innershiv.js"></script>
<![endif]-->
```

The innershim and innerShiv files work together to allow you to work with HTML5 on older versions of IE.

Notice that each of these additions is contained within conditional comments that target IE versions earlier than version 8. This is to avoid unnecessary adding and processing of scripts for browsers that don't need them.

<SCRIPT>

The meaning and usage of the script element hasn't changed at all in HTML5. However, because a good part of this book is about JavaScript APIs, it's worth noting one new and useful difference: You no longer have to specify the type attribute if you are using it to enclose JavaScript.

Yes, the clever people at the WHATWG and the W3C have decided that by default type="text/javascript ', which prevents you from having to type it and makes for much neater code:

```
<script>
    alert("I didn't have to specify the type attribute!");
</script>
```

WRAPPING UP

The processes involved for the current HTML5 specifications to arrive at where they are now were of course quite a bit more complicated than has been described in this chapter. But the brief explanation should give you a foundation in the process.

In addition, the elements mentioned are only a very small portion of the new elements contained in the HTML5 specification, and there have also been changes made to elements that existed in HTML 4.01 and earlier versions. You can read a full list of these differences at www.w3.org/TR/html5-diff.

However, the elements you encountered in this chapter are sufficient for you to create your own simple HTML5 documents. This knowledge will also aid your understanding of the examples and resources provided in this book.

In the next chapter, you'll learn a bit about the history of multimedia within browsers, and you'll also take a close look at the HTML5 elements that are specifically relevant to HTML5 multimedia.

2

HTML5 **MULTIMEDIA ELEMENTS**

Now that you're armed with the basic history of HTML5 and its structural elements, you can start learning about HTML5 multimedia, its elements, their attributes, and the combined functionality that they bring.

HTML 4.01 had no defined method of bringing audio and video to a website, which led to a huge popularity in third-party plugins, such as Flash, to deliver multimedia content. But HTML5 provides this much-needed structure to deliver audio and video across the Internet through a web browser.

This chapter offers some history of multimedia in the browser and how the playback of audio and video was achieved through the many applications, players, and plugins that various vendors released. Then you'll learn about the new HTML5 elements, which let you to take advantage of native multimedia in the browser.

HISTORY OF WEB MULTIMEDIA

When browsers and the idea of the web first appeared back in the early 1990s, there wasn't any web multimedia. Soon thereafter, images began to be incorporated but were at best a poor man's multimedia. Although they could be animated with the advent of animated GIFs, they were of course completely noninteractive.

Even with the existence of audio and video files, the ability of internet technology to deliver this multimedia across the web was limited. Internet connections were slow, audio and video files were large, and no one wanted to wait for large files to download. Once the file did arrive, an external player had to be used to view the contents, which was separate from the web browser. This was the norm, and few complained.

The phenomenal increase in internet connection speeds brought with it the ability to send multimedia across the web even faster, and web browser technology had to move just as quickly, which of course it did with the introduction of what's now referred to as *native multimedia*.

Before you dive into native multimedia, let's quickly take a look at an overview of the external players that were (and still are as desktop players) used to play back audio and video files.

MEDIA PLAYERS

A media player is a standard term used to describe a piece of software that has the capability of playing back multimedia files, such as audio and video, usually via a graphical user interface.

In the mid-1990s, the MIDI (Musical Instrument Digital Interface) file format was used to play background music on web documents, and the music usually played automatically. Although highly annoying, this was the beginning of multimedia becoming available through the browser. A host of other players from different vendors were then developed to infest your computer.

RealNetworks released its audio player RealAudio back in 1995, which first introduced the idea of playing audio through the web using proprietary .ra and .ram audio files. Further developments of RealAudio led to the release of RealVideo in 1997, which allowed video streaming and was based on the H.263 video format. These two players eventually were bundled together under the RealPlayer name and were included in Windows 98 as a selectable tool. RealPlayer is still around today (version 14 is the latest stable release) and is available across many platforms; it is capable of playing multiple audio and video file formats.

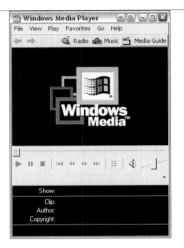

FIGURE 2.1 Microsoft Media Player 6 shipped with Windows 98.

Macromedia released its first edition of Shockwave in 1995, which was originally developed for the Netscape web browser. At the time, the company allowed users of its popular Director multimedia software to create interactive applications and animations, and insert them into a web document. Macromedia also had another media player in development; it released the Shockwave Flash player in 2002, which supported video as well as audio. Shockwave Flash player used the SWF file format developed by FutureWave software. The main intent of the SWF file format was to create small files for displaying animations, as well as to use it to exchange audio, video, and data. Macromedia was bought by Adobe in 2005, and the Shockwave Flash player was renamed Adobe Flash. It is this particular player that became the player to use when delivering multimedia through the browser.

Microsoft improved on its previous offerings and released DirectShow in 1996, which later became Media Player 6.1 and was released as part of Windows 98 (**Figure 2.1**).

With the release of Windows 2000, Microsoft also released version 7.1 of Windows Media Player. This had a much improved graphical interface and overall offered a better experience. With this release came *codecs*—special file protocols that allow for creating and playing back media content.

NOTE: You'll read more about codecs in Chapters 3 and 4 on HTML5 audio and video, respectively.

With subsequent releases, Microsoft enhanced its Media Player, continuously improving the offering along the way.

Microsoft also worked on an application framework to rival Adobe Flash in that it could run browser *plugins* (sets of small software components that add specific abilities to other, larger software applications—in this case a web browser) and other rich internet applications. Initially released in 2007, Microsoft Silverlight supported many different types of audio and video file formats, as well as animation and interactivity. Originally, it had a slow adoption rate, but as of June 2011, it had roughly 73 percent market penetration, with Adobe Flash holding at 97 percent market share.

Apple was also in the multimedia player game from the early days. Its first version of QuickTime was released in 1991 for the System Software 6 operating system. QuickTime continued to be a Mac-only piece of software until the release of QuickTime 4.0 in 1999, which also ran on Windows and supported MP3 audio playback. QuickTime 5 and 6 delivered video and Flash playback, with version 6 also supporting MP4 playback. Release 7 came out in 2005 and had improved MP4 playback but dropped support for Flash content. The latest version of QuickTime at the time of this writing is version 10 for the Mac OS, and different flavours of Microsoft Windows have earlier versions.

Every vendor had its own way of delivering multimedia, but of course none were perfect. There was no standardised method of embedding audio and video into a web document, and it is for this reason—to standardise embedding of multimedia— that the audio and video elements became part of the HTML5 specification.

ISSUES WITH MEDIA PLAYERS

All of the media players had one major problem in common: End users needed to have the appropriate plugin installed to be able to play the required audio or video.

Initially, all these plugins did was launch the respective media player to play the audio or video. The ability to display multimedia within the browser came later, although pop-ups (where the appropriate media player was started outside of the browser) were still common. If the required plugin did not exist on your system, you had to download it, which was a hassle because you needed to constantly update it.

In addition, different plugins from different vendors could conflict with each other, causing browser instability. For example, the VLC Media Player conflicts with the Windows Media Player in Firefox, sometimes causing Firefox to crash when attempting to view a WMV file.

Security was also an issue, because plugins were and still are one of the main target areas for malware. An example of this was identified in March 2011 when it was determined that a critical vulnerability in Flash Player 10.2 could allow remote attackers to execute arbitrary code or cause a denial of service attack on the infected machine (see www.adobe.com/support/security/advisories/apsa11-01.html).

Of course as soon as these vulnerabilities are detected, the vendors move quickly to patch them and push out a release. But again this means that the user must constantly upgrade to the latest versions when they become available.

One major issue with the most popular plugin of them all, Flash, is Apple's April 2010 decision not to support Flash on iPhones and iPads. This of course makes content served in Flash completely unavailable on these devices.

Let's now look at how these media players could be harnessed through their plugins to play the required audio or video in HTML.

HTML ELEMENTS

In the past, to embed plugins within your web document to launch a media player, you could use various HTML elements to do so. Although using these elements is the way it was done in the past, you still need to be aware of these elements and how they are used, because unfortunately, not all browsers support HTML5 multimedia. You'll read more about this lack of browser support for HTML5 multimedia in Chapters 3 and 4.

In fact, three different HTML elements could be used:

- applet
- embed
- object

The applet element, as its name suggests, was only ever used for embedding Java applets and was actually deprecated in HTML 4.01. It allowed a Java applet to be embedded anywhere within the web document where the element was placed. Most likely, you'll never need to use this element because it's now obsolete, so let's move on.

The embed element was introduced by the Netscape 2.0 browser to allow developers to embed an arbitrary data object within a web document. If the required plugin was not installed on your system, a warning was usually displayed along with an empty box. An example of embed code being used to play a MIDI file looks like this:

```
<embed src="myMidiFile.mid" height="60" width="144">
```

Here the browser is being told to embed the myMidiFile.mid into the browser at the specified position with the specified dimensions.

NOTE: The embed element was officially introduced in HTML5, finally making it a valid part of an HTML specification. Although most browsers supported it prior to HTML5, it was never actually a valid element.

The object element replaced the applet and embed elements (neither were ever actually in any specification) in HTML 4.01 and was intended to be more generic with regards to the media that it contains. Therefore, it can be used to embed Java applets, audio, and video. The object element is quite powerful in that it can accept a large number of arguments and data object types, but this in turn renders it rather unwieldy. The following example shows how the object element can be used to embed an Adobe Flash video file:

```
<object type="application/x-shockwave-flash" width="512"
→ height="300" wmode="transparent" data="flvplayer.swf?
→ file=myFlashVideo.flv&autoStart=true">

    <param name="movie" value="flvplayer.swf?file=
    → myFlashVideo.flv&autoStart=true" />

    <param name="wmode" value="transparent" />

    <param name="allowscriptaccess" value="always" />

    <param name="allowfullscreen" value="always" />
</object>
```

The code here indicates to the browser that the content within the object element is Flash via the MIME (Multipurpose Internet Mail Extension) type in the type attribute. It also sets the width and height of the object container, and uses the wmode attribute to inform the browser that the background of the HTML page should show through on transparent sections of the Flash content. The data attribute is used to point to a valid URL, which will contain the actual content of the container.

The param element is used to add different parameters to the embedded content. As you can see, one of the param elements here is used to set a parameter called movie whose value is the same as the data attribute set in the overall object element! This leads to duplication, which is, sadly, necessary. This is a fallback: If the browser doesn't know how to play objects with a MIME type of application/ x-shockwave-flash, it will check the next child element and see if it can play that (in this case, the param setting for movie).

The wmode parameter is also set again for browsers that don't understand the first setting in the object declaration. Two other parameters are set: allowscriptaccess, which allows the HTML page to interact with the object should the object have anything to interact with; and allowfullscreen, which allows the object to fill the full screen should the user request it.

You might agree that the preceding code is a bit painful and confusing to look at initially. Fortunately, HTML5 makes embedding of multimedia objects much easier because multimedia is now native to the browser.

WELCOME, NATIVE MULTIMEDIA!

With native multimedia, the object is no longer embedded into the web document but is treated as a native object by the browser and therefore built in. This provides immediate benefits, such as:

- Plugins are no longer required.
- Speed—anything native to a browser will be faster than any third-party add-on.
- Native controls are provided by the browser.
- Keyboard accessibility is built in automatically.

HTML5 provides four new markup elements that help you to achieve native multimedia in the browser. Let's take a look at each of these elements and their possible attributes.

THE AUDIO ELEMENT

The audio element allows you to embed audio files or an audio stream into a web document. Here's a quick piece of code showing you just how much easier it is to embed an audio file in your web document using the audio element:

```
<audio src="sayHello.mp3"></audio>
```

Much simpler, isn't it?

Table 2.1 lists the attributes that the element can take.

TABLE 2.1 Audio Element Attributes

ATTRIBUTE	DESCRIPTION
src	Provides the address of the media resource, in this case an audio file or stream. This attribute must contain a valid URL to the audio source.
preload	Is used to hint to the browser how to preload the audio source, if at all. It only advises the browser what to do, but ultimately the browser will do what it wants (e.g., based on a user setting). It has three possible settings: • **none** — Informs the browser not to preload the audio file. The user is not expected to play the audio, so there's no need to perform any preloading. It will begin to load as soon as the user clicks the Play button. • **metadata** — Informs the browser to only preload information about the audio file (e.g., dimensions, duration, etc.). The user may want to play the audio. Its metadata (e.g., dimensions, duration) should be preloaded. The rest of the audio will download when the user clicks the Play button. • **auto** — Tells the browser to decide whether to download the metadata, the entire source, or not to download anything. This is the default if preload is not specified. Support for this attribute is poor; only Firefox 5 and Chrome 12 currently support it.

TABLE 2.1 Audio Element Attributes *(continued)*

ATTRIBUTE	DESCRIPTION
autoplay	Is a boolean attribute that informs the browser to automatically start playing the audio source when the page is loaded. Use this with caution because autoplaying audio can be an annoyance to users.
controls	Is also a boolean attribute, which if present, tells the browser to provide a default set of controls for the audio.
muted	Controls the default state of the audio source. Naturally, this is largely redundant with an audio source because if you play it automatically, you'll want it heard. Currently no browser supports this attribute.
loop	Another boolean attribute, which indicates that the audio is to be continuously played in a loop. It's advisable to use this with caution because it can be an annoyance to users, especially if you don't provide any controls for them to stop it! This attribute is currently not supported in Firefox 5.
crossorigin	Is a relatively new attribute to the specification that is intended to allow or prohibit cross-origin media of the audio source using the CORS (Cross-Origin Resource Sharing) specification (which you can read about at www.w3.org/TR/cors). Basically, it specifies whether the audio source can be shared across other domains. It can have two settings: • **anonymous** — Allows anonymous access to the audio source. • **use-credentials** — Credentials are required to access the audio source. If no particular setting is specified, but crossorigin is present, it defaults to the anonymous setting. Because this attribute is so new to the specification, it is yet to be implemented in any of the major browsers.
mediagroup	Allows multiple media elements, in this case audio sources, to be linked together. This can, for example, allow the playing and synchronisation of two different audio sources in two different places on the screen.

FIGURE 2.2 The audio controls in Firefox 5.

FIGURE 2.3 The audio controls in Safari 5.0.5.

FIGURE 2.4 The audio controls in Chrome 12.

FIGURE 2.5 The audio controls in Opera 11.50.

FIGURE 2.6 The audio controls in Internet Explorer 9.

As you can see in Table 2.1, several different settings can be used with the audio element, some of which have a number of settings. A sample audio declaration in a web document might look like this:

```
<audio src="sayHello.ogg" controls></audio>
```

This simple piece of code informs the browser to embed the specified audio file in the browser and to use the browser's own multimedia controls. Various browsers have different default controls, so how the audio controls look depends on the browser that the viewer is using. You can see examples of how these controls are rendered differently in **Figures 2.2** through **2.6**.

You'll learn more about the audio element in Chapter 3. More in-depth examples of its usage are provided as well as how to combine most of the attributes listed in Table 2.1.

Now that you've taken a quick look at the attributes of the audio element, let's check out the video element.

THE VIDEO ELEMENT

The video element allows you to embed video content into your web document, and once again you can specify a number of attributes to control this video content.

Many attributes are the same as those specified for the audio element, but there are some extras, and they're all listed in **Table 2.2**.

TABLE 2.2 Video Element Attributes

ATTRIBUTE	DESCRIPTION
src	Provides the address of the media resource, in this case a video file or stream. This attribute must contain a valid URL to the video source.
preload	Is used to hint to the browser how to preload the video source, if at all. Again, it's only a hint to the browser, which may choose to override it with a possible user setting.
	It has three possible settings:
	• none — Informs the browser that the user is not expected to want to view the video, so there's no need to perform any preloading.
	• metadata — Informs the browser that the user may want to view the video, and therefore its metadata (e.g., dimensions, duration) should be preloaded.
	• auto — Tells the browser to decide whether to download the metadata, the entire source, or not to download anything. This is the default if preload is not specified.
autoplay	Is a boolean attribute that informs the browser to automatically start playing the video source as soon as it can. It's not considered good practice to do this!
controls	Is also a boolean attribute, which if present, tells the browser to provide a default set of controls for the video.
muted	Controls the default state of the video source. This means that you can specify that an automatically playing video can be muted when it begins to play, thus preventing any irritation to the user.
	This attribute is currently not supported in any of the major browsers.
loop	Another boolean attribute, which indicates that the video is to be continuously played in a loop.
	This is currently not supported in Firefox 5.
poster	Allows an image file to be displayed when there's no video data available.
	If poster is not specified, the browser will display the first frame from the video, which may of course not be the image that you want shown. It must contain a valid URL to the image in question.

TABLE 2.2 Video Element Attributes *(continued)*

ATTRIBUTE	DESCRIPTION
width	Specifies the width of the video element in pixels.
height	Specifies the height of the video element in pixels.
crossorigin	Indicates whether the video source can be shared across domains or not. By default, the source can be shared cross-domain. It can have two settings: • **anonymous** — Allows anonymous access to the video source. • **use-credentials** — Credentials are required to access the video source. If no particular setting is specified, but crossorigin is present, it defaults to the anonymous setting. Because this attribute is so new to the specification, it is yet to be implemented in any of the browsers
mediagroup	Allows multiple media elements, in this case video sources, to be linked together. This can, for example, allow the playing and synchronisation of two different videos in two different places on the screen.

CROSSORIGIN

crossorigin is a very recent addition to the HTML5 specification, and as such, currently has no real-world application. None of the major browsers support it. It uses the CORS (Cross-Origin Resource Sharing) specification, which you can read about at www.w3.org/TR/cors.

MEDIAGROUP

Like crossorigin, mediagroup is a very new addition to the HTML5 specification and at the time of this writing hasn't been implemented in any of the major browsers yet. Once implemented, it will be very useful for accessibility, because it allows scenarios such as playing a sign-language video alongside a regular video and keeps them in sync.

FIGURE 2.7 The video controls in Firefox 5.

FIGURE 2.8 The video controls in Safari 5.0.5.

FIGURE 2.9 The video controls in Chrome 12.

FIGURE 2.10 The video controls in Opera 11.50.

FIGURE 2.11 The video controls in Internet Explorer 9.

As you can see, many of the audio and video elements' attributes are the same, which of course makes it that much easier when specifying them because you only need to remember one set of attributes.

An example of using the video element to display a video in a web document complete with browser controls might look like this:

```
<video src="snowy-tree.mp4" width="300" height="176" controls>
→ </video>
```

This simple example informs the browser to display a video player of size 300 pixels by 176 pixels with default media controls containing the snowy-tree.mp4 video file.

As with audio, various browsers display the controls and video differently. You can see how they look in each browser in **Figures 2.7** through **2.11**.

THE SOURCE ELEMENT

Due to different browser requirements (more on this in Chapters 3 and 4), it is often required that you specify different sources for the same audio or video element.

As you saw earlier, both the audio and video elements provide a src attribute in which to place a URL to the audio or video source. But that attribute only allows for one source. So how can you add multiple sources?

This is where the source element comes in. Any number of source elements can be contained within an audio or video element declaration, and it is through this element that you can specify multiple media sources.

The source element can contain the attributes listed in **Table 2.3**.

So the source element allows you to specify different sources for a particular multimedia offering, an example of which follows:

```
<audio controls>
    <source src="sayHello.ogg" type="audio/ogg">
    <source src="sayHello.mp3" type="audio/mp3">
    Sorry, your browser doesn't support the audio element
</audio>
```

In this example, two different audio file formats are presented to the browser for it to play. The browser will play the first format it recognises and ignore any formats that it doesn't recognise. If it can't find a format that it can play, it will inform the user that the browser is unable to play the audio by displaying the text, "Sorry, your browser doesn't support the audio element."

This process of a browser ignoring what it can't understand proves very useful when serving up a multimedia solution for cross-browser support. As mentioned earlier, different browsers support different multimedia file formats, which you'll read about in more detail in the next two chapters.

TABLE 2.3 Source Element Attributes

ATTRIBUTE	DESCRIPTION
src	Provides the address of the media resource, be it audio or video. As with the src attribute of the audio and video elements, this must contain a valid URL to the source in question.
type	Specifies the type of the media resource to aid the browser in determining if it can actually play this source or not. The value must be a valid MIME type, which tells the browser what format the source is in.
	The most common include:
	• audio/ogg • audio/mp3 • video/mp4 • video/ogg • video/webm
	In some cases, the codec that the source is encoded with may also need to be specified to ensure that it can be played. You'll learn more about MIME type and codecs in Chapters 3 and 4.
media	Specifies the intended media type of the resource in question, because it might target a certain type of device with a certain height, width, resolution, or aspect ratio.
	This value must be a valid media query. You can read more about this attribute in the media queries specification at http://dev.w3.org/csswg/css3-mediaqueries.
	You'll learn more about media queries and their uses in Chapter 4.

THE TRACK ELEMENT

The track element is used to specify explicit external timed text tracks for media elements. It must be used in conjunction with either an audio or video element because it doesn't represent anything on its own.

This element is mainly used to provide increased accessibility to a multimedia resource, because it allows captions, descriptions, transcripts, and subtitles to be provided. These can then be displayed in the browser in conjunction with the media being played.

In most cases, the information provided through the track element is more suited to a video media source.

Like the other elements described earlier, the track element can take a number of attributes (**Table 2.4**).

The track element can therefore be used to specify complete transcriptions of media resources, which, for example, can be useful in making the source available to those with auditory impairments. It also allows you to specify multiple subtitles and descriptions in different languages. Here is an example:

```
<video src="sayHello.mp4">

    <track kind="subtitles" src="hello-en.vtt" srclang="en"
    →  label="English">

    <track kind="subtitles" src="hello-de.vtt" srclang="de"
    →  label="German">

</video>
```

This example specifies two different files for the sayHello.mp4 video for two different languages, English and German.

NOTE: HTML5 video and subtitles are discussed in detail in Chapter 8, so don't fret!

TABLE 2.4 Track Element Attributes

ATTRIBUTE	DESCRIPTION
kind	Specifies what type of data this instance of the track element provides for the specified media element. It can have any of the following values:
	• subtitles — A full transcription of the dialogue, which is suitable for use when the audio is available but not understood. The contents will be displayed as an overlay on the video.
	• captions — A transcription of the dialogue, sound effects, and other relevant audio information, and is suitable when the audio/soundtrack is unavailable. The contents are overlayed on the video and are labeled as useful for those with auditory impairments.
	• descriptions — Provides textual descriptions of the video component of the media resource and is intended for when the visual component is unavailable.
	• chapters — Specifies chapter titles and is used to navigate the contents of the media resource.
	• metadata — Contains information that is to be used via a script and is not actually displayed on the browser in any way.
	If this attribute is omitted, the default value is subtitles.
src	Provides the address of the text track data, which must be a valid URL. The file provided at this source needs to be in a specific format for it to be understood—two of which are WebSRT and WebVTT. Both formats are discussed in Chapter 8.
srclang	Indicates the language of the text track data.
label	Specifies a user-readable title for the track, which provides a more understandable title for the user to read. Must be unique across track elements of the same kind attribute for the same resource.
default	Informs the browser that the track element in question is to be used as the default if the user's preferences do not indicate that a different one would be more appropriate.

A **QUIRK** OF **SAFARI** AND **INTERNET EXPLORER 9**

Earlier in the chapter when I mentioned that native multimedia is the bee's knees and that it doesn't require third-party plugins, which is ideal, I might have been bending the truth a little. It's not to say that native multimedia isn't great, it is; it's wonderful.

But.

For native multimedia to work in Safari and Internet Explorer 9, Apple has decided that you must have its QuickTime plugin installed, and Microsoft requires you to install its Media Player on your system.

These requirements somewhat detract from the idea of native multimedia. Why Apple and Microsoft have chosen to take this path I don't know, but this is the way of things as they stand.

WRAPPING **UP**

You've taken a brief look back at the availability of multimedia within the web browser. Predictably, the technology involved and the results that can be achieved have advanced a great deal from the days of "images only."

You also are now aware of the three new HTML5 markup elements—audio, video, and source—that you'll need to embed audio and video content into your web document. The track element was included because it provides you with a powerful method to make your media content accessible by allowing you to specify enhancements, such as subtitles and captions.

With this grounding in the elements and their attributes under your belt, you'll next learn how to use these elements to bring media to your users.

With no further ado, let's move on to the next chapter and explore what you can do with HTML5 audio.

3

USING **AUDIO**

Adding native audio to your web document using HTML5 multimedia couldn't be easier. Whether you wanted to share sound snippets, voice recordings, or your own music with users on the Internet, the ability to do so was always available. But now you can share audio without having to rely on third-party plugins being installed.

Chapter 2 introduced you to the HTML5 elements and attributes that allow you to add audio to your web document. Now it's time to explore how this is actually done. This chapter explains, with the aid of examples, how you can use these elements and attributes.

But let's first take a brief look at the audio file formats that are available for use and how you might convert existing audio from one format to another to use in your web document.

AUDIO CODECS AND FILE FORMATS

The plethora of different plugins and formats that are available for encoding multimedia files for presentation on the web could cause a bit of a headache if the particular plugin or audio codec isn't available on a user's system.

HANG ON; WHAT'S AN AUDIO CODEC?

A codec is a computer program that uses a compression algorithm to encode and/or decode (hence the name: coder-decoder) a digital stream of data, making it more suitable for playback on a computer or other device.

The objective of the codec is usually to maintain the high quality of the audio signal using the smallest number of bits possible to reduce the size of the file in question and hence the bandwidth required for transfer.

Different audio codecs can be used to output different audio file formats—a number of which are supported by HTML5.

OGG VORBIS

Ogg Vorbis is an open source, unpatented, free file format created by the Xiph. Org Foundation (www.xiph.org). Because it is free of charge, it tends to be quite attractive as a format to use.

Ogg is the name of the container format, and Vorbis is the specific audio compression it uses. According to the Vorbis website (www.vorbis.com), Vorbis files can compress to a small file size and yet still maintain good sound quality. This of course is ideal for delivery across the web because it reduces bandwidth costs.

The Ogg Vorbis format has proved quite popular among the gaming community with companies like Epic Games, Crystal Dynamics, and EA Games using it to deliver game music.

Ogg Vorbis uses the application/ogg MIME type and audio/ogg codec.

MP3

MP3 has rather a misleading name because it's also known as MPEG-1 or MPEG-2 Audio Layer III. Developed by the Moving Picture Expert Group (www.mpeg.org), MP3 differs from Ogg Vorbis in that it is covered under a patent held by Fraunhofer (www.fraunhofer.de/en), which receives a percentage of each sale.

The MP3 standard does not actually include an exact specification on how to encode MP3, but the standard does specify how to decode the format. This of course has resulted in many different MP3 encoders, each of which produces audio files of different sound quality.

Despite the patent, MP3 has proved to be one of the most popular audio formats for encoding sound files.

MP3 uses the audio/mpeg MIME type and audio/mp3 codec.

WAV

The WAV file format's proper name is Waveform Audio File Format but is called WAV due to its file extension. WAV is an audio format that was first created by Microsoft and IBM in 1991.

Although it can contain compressed data, it usually doesn't, which of course can render rather large file sizes. It is for this reason that its use as a format for delivering audio over the internet has declined.

WAV uses the `audio/wav` MIME type and `audio/wav` codec.

AAC

Advanced Audio Coding (AAC) is an audio format used by Apple and has been made popular as the default format for Apple's iTunes Store. It was designed to be the successor to the MP3 format and for this reason usually has a better sound quality than MP3.

AAC uses the `audio/aac` MIME type and `audio/aac` codec.

MP4

Although mainly used as a video file format (more on that in Chapter 4), MP4 can also be used to encode audio only. Like AAC, it has been made popular by Apple, which also uses it to encode some audio files with the `.m4a` extension.

MP4 uses the `audio/mp4` MIME type and `audio/mp4` codec.

Now that you know about the different audio formats, let's look at how they are supported across browsers.

BROWSER SUPPORT FOR
AUDIO FORMATS

When the first drafts of the HTML5 specification came out, they included a recommendation, nay, a requirement, that all web browsers must have built-in support for the Ogg Vorbis audio format. This was beneficial because you could be guaranteed that each browser that supported the HTML5 audio element would at least support Ogg Vorbis, and you could present your audio file in that format.

However, this utopia of a universally supported audio format changed when both Apple and Nokia objected to this requirement. Apple simply didn't want any compulsory requirement for a technology that, at the time, wasn't widely supported (plus Apple had a vested interest in the MP4 file format), whereas Nokia claimed that the Ogg Vorbis format wasn't as open and free as it claimed.

As a result, the requirement was removed from the specification. Consequently, different vendors decided to support different audio codecs. **Table 3.1** contains a list of which vendors support certain audio formats in their browsers.

TABLE 3.1 Audio Formats and Browser Support

FORMAT	BROWSER				
Ogg Vorbis	Firefox 3.5–	Chrome 5+	Opera 10.5+		
MP3	Safari 5+	Chrome 6+	IE9+	iOS	
WAV	Firefox 3.6+	Chrome 8+	Safari 5+	Opera 10.5+	
AAC	Safari 3+	Chrome 5+	IE9+	iOS 3+	Android 2+
MP4	Safari 3+	Chrome 5+	IE9+	iOS 3+	Android 2+

NOTE: Chrome is due to drop support for MP4/H.264. See http://blog.chromium.org/2011/01/more-about-chrome-html-video-codec.html for more information.

Browser support of audio formats is a bit of a mixed bag, but you can easily combat this by presenting the audio file in the different formats required using the audio and source elements you read about in Chapter 2.

With different browsers supporting different formats, you must be wondering how to convert from one format to another. Well, let's take a quick look.

ENCODING YOUR AUDIO FILE

Once you have your audio file, whether you recorded it yourself or obtained it from elsewhere, it will generally be in one format only. Most likely, it will be in one of the formats mentioned earlier, but it might not be.

You could of course decide to support only one audio type. You might know, for example, that all your users will use Firefox, and therefore you only have to support Ogg Vorbis.

For argument's sake, let's say that you want to support all the main browsers, so you need to convert your audio file to the other formats. How do you do this?

Well, many encoders will do the job for you, and most of them are free. Here are two of my favourite encoders for converting the various audio formats from one to another:

- **Miro Video Converter** (www.mirovideoconverter.com) allows you to open many different audio file formats and convert them to MP3, WAV, Ogg, and others via a simple drag-and-drop interface. It runs on both Windows and Mac.

- **Media Converter** (www.mediaconverter.org) is an online conversion application that allows you to either upload an audio file or use one that's already online. It also allows you to convert your audio file to MP3, WAV, and Ogg.

Many other encoders are of course available, but I prefer these two because one is a desktop application and one is online. This suits all occasions because the desktop application is useful when I am offline, and of course the web converter is useful when I want a quick file conversion and am online.

However, you must face a particular issue if you want to support browsers that do not have HTML5 multimedia-playing capabilities.

TIP: It's a good idea to have a number of your favourite converters either on your desktop/laptop or online so that you can always convert between the different formats at will when you need to. Although only two have been mentioned here, you may find different encoders that you prefer.

LEGACY BROWSER FALLBACK

The eagle-eyed among you will have noticed that at no stage yet have I brought up Internet Explorer 6 to 8. As mentioned in Chapter 2, these browsers don't support any HTML5 and need JavaScript help in order for them to render the elements. And it gets slightly worse with regard to multimedia, because naturally there is no native support for any of the aforementioned audio file formats.

So what's the solution? You use a method that the Internet Explorer versions *do* understand, which means Flash, QuickTime, or some other third-party plugin. Or, you simply provide a link to the audio file in question so that any unlucky users can download the file and play it in the old style via an audio player on their computers. This is achieved by using the audio and source elements.

A complete example of how to use the audio and source elements to do this, along with how to provide Flash fallback is provided in the next section, as well as other examples on how to use the audio element.

EXAMPLES OF USING THE AUDIO ELEMENT

By now you've read enough about HTML5 audio and are eager to see some proper examples of how to actually use it in a web document. Well, here you'll do just that.

All the elements and attributes that are used in the code in this section were introduced to you in Chapter 2.

PLAYING AN AUDIO FILE

If you want to simply play an audio file, you just need to use an instance of the audio element. For example, to allow the user to play an Ogg Vorbis audio file, you simply use this:

```
<audio src="sayHello.ogg" controls></audio>
```

The `controls` attribute tells the browser to display its default controls to users to allow them to control the playback of the file.

However, if you were evil and wanted to play the file before your users had a chance to do anything about it, you would add the `autoplay` attribute:

```
<audio src="sayHello.ogg" controls autoplay></audio>
```

If you were even more evil, you could play the audio file to users automatically and in a loop, like this:

```
<audio src="sayHello.ogg" controls autoplay loop></audio>
```

And if you had some vendetta against your users and wanted to torment them, you could remove the `controls` attribute, thus rendering them unable to stop the playback:

```
<audio src="sayHello.ogg" autoplay loop></audio>
```

NOTE: You can find all of the examples (and more) in this section on the accompanying website at www.html5multimedia.com.

Note that I am not recommending that you use autoplay or loop, or remove the controls attribute. It's generally not a nice thing to do and can really annoy your users. Just ensure that you can justify your decision should you decide to use autoplay or loop.

You can also mute the file when it first loads by using the muted attribute. This specifies the default state of the audio, which you might want to do to potentially override any user preferences:

```
<audio src="sayHello.ogg" controls autoplay muted></audio>
```

In addition, you can request that the browser not preload the audio file on startup. The previous examples all default to preload="auto" when it's not specified:

```
<audio src="sayHello.ogg" controls preload="none"></audio>
```

And of course you can request that the browser load the metadata only. This can be apt when the audio file is quite long or you know that the user may actually choose not to listen to the audio file:

```
<audio src="sayHello.ogg" controls preload="metadata"></audio>
```

Any use of the preload attribute is simply a suggestion to the browser and may actually be overridden by the browser itself, perhaps based on a user setting.

All the preceding examples use just one audio source. So what if you need to serve up multiple sources for different browsers?

PLAYING AN AUDIO FILE WITH DIFFERENT SOURCES

Let's say you wanted to provide audio in both Ogg Vorbis and MP3 formats to support Firefox, Chrome, Opera, Safari, and IE9. You can do this by using the source element in conjunction with the audio element. The code would look like this:

```
<audio controls>
    <source src="sayHello.ogg" type="audio/ogg">
    <source src="sayHello.mp3" type="audio/mp3">
</audio>
```

It couldn't be easier!

Naturally, you can add a WAV file format too (should you want to):

```
<audio controls>
    <source src="sayHello.ogg" type="audio/ogg">
    <source src="sayHello.mp3" type="audio/mp3">
    <source src="sayHello.wav" type="audio/wav">
</audio>
```

You can incorporate any of the attributes mentioned earlier here as well. So making whichever source the browser chooses to play automatically would simply require this code:

```
<audio controls autoplay>
    <source src="sayHello.ogg" type="audio/ogg">
    <source src="sayHello.mp3" type="audio/mp3">
    <source src="sayHello.wav" type="audio/wav">
</audio>
```

To support browsers that don't support the HTML5 audio element, you'd follow the same tactic, but the fallback is different.

PLAYING AN AUDIO FILE WITH DIFFERENT
SOURCES AND LEGACY FALLBACK

Because legacy browsers like Internet Explorer 6 to 8 don't support HTML5, if you want to support these browsers (and you should), you need to revert to another format that they do understand—something like Flash for example.

So, do you need to pollute your nice, clean, HTML5 markup with ugly Flash plugin code? Yes, I'm afraid you do unless you are happy with simply providing a link to the audio file for the user to download.

In much the same way as HTML5-supporting browsers work their way through the sources your document presents to them to find an audio format they can play, legacy browsers will ignore all these audio formats until they come across a file they can play, be it a Flash file, or whatever.

There are a number of ways you can provide Flash file playback: via a Flash player that you host on your server; by using a remote Flash player, such as Google's Flash Player; or by using either the embed or object elements (see Chapter 2).

The code for using a downloaded player (this particular player is the Google Flash Player already mentioned, which I have simply downloaded) and the object element might look like this:

```
<audio controls>
    <source src="sayHello.ogg" type="audio/ogg">
    <source src="sayHello.mp3" type="audio/mp3">
    <object type="application/x-shockwave-flash"
        data="player.swf?audioUrl=sayHello.mp3&autoPlay=true"
        height="27" width="320">
        <param name="movie"
        value="player.swf?audioUrl=sayHello.mp3&autoPlay=true">
    </object>
</audio>
```

TIP: You can download the excellent JW Player, a Flash player from Longtail Video, at www.longtailvideo.com/players/jw-flv-player. Although JW Player is a complete HTML5 and Flash Video player solution, it does contain a Flash player within the downloaded ZIP file (player.swf) that you can use.

The same code using the embed element looks like this:

```
<audio controls>
    <source src="sayHello.ogg" type="audio/ogg">
    <source src="sayHello.mp3" type="audio/mp3">
    <embed type="application/x-shockwave-flash"
        wmode="transparent"
        src="player.swf?audioUrl=sayHello.mp3&autoPlay=true"
        height="27"
        width="320">
</audio>
```

And using Google's Flash Player and the embed element looks like this:

```
<audio controls>
    <source src="sayHello.ogg" type="audio/ogg">
    <source src="sayHello.mp3" type="audio/mp3">
    <embed type="application/x-shockwave-flash"
        wmode="transparent"
        src="http://www.google.com/reader/ui/3523697345-audio-
        ⤳ player.swf?audioUrl=sayHello.mp3&autoPlay=true"
        height="27"
        width="320">
</audio>
```

FIGURE 3.1 The audio player in Firefox 5.

FIGURE 3.2 A sample Flash player as viewed in Internet Explorer 8.

All of the preceding examples will work in browsers that support HTML5 audio, as shown in Firefox in **Figure 3.1**.

And the examples will all work in Internet Explorer 8 using a Flash player, as shown in **Figure 3.2**.

You can take advantage of the fact that Flash can play MP3 files, so you don't have to serve up yet another audio file format. Of course, users must have the Flash player installed on their system. But what if they don't?

Well, you can go one step further with the fallbacks presented and offer a simple link to the file for the user to download:

```
<audio controls>
    <source src="sayHello.ogg" type="audio/ogg">
    <source src="sayHello.mp3" type="audio/mp3">
    <object type="application/x-shockwave-flash"
        data="player.swf?audioUrl=sayHello.mp3&autoPlay=true"
        height="27" width="320">
        <param name="movie"
        value="player.swf?audioUrl=sayHello.mp3&autoPlay=true">
    </object>
    <a href="sayHello.mp3">Download the audio file</a>
</audio>
```

FIGURE 3.3 Internet Explorer 8 showing the Flash player as well as the download link to the audio file.

FIGURE 3.4 Firefox displays an ugly box if it is unable to play any of the HTML5 audio files provided.

If the browser doesn't support HTML5 audio but does have the Flash plugin installed, it will display both the Flash player and the link, as shown in **Figure 3.3**. This isn't necessarily a bad thing of course, and in fact you might want to always provide a download link for the user.

If you decide not to support Flash, you can omit the Flash embed element and provide the hyperlink to download the file only:

```
<audio controls>
    <source src="sayHello.ogg" type="audio/ogg">
    <source src="sayHello.mp3" type="audio/mp3">
    <a href="sayHello.mp3">Download the audio file</a>
</audio>
```

You should also provide file formats for browsers that *do* support HTML5 audio playback. If the browser does support HTML5 but is unable to play any of the sources provided, it won't revert to playing any Flash content you may also have provided nor display the download link should one be present. Instead, a broken player might be displayed, or as in the case of Firefox, a rather ugly black box (**Figure 3.4**).

Whatever you decide to do, there are enough fallback mechanisms available to help you support most browsers.

WRAPPING **UP**

At the moment, the major web browsers support different audio file formats, which require your audio content to be provided in the various formats in order for these browsers to be able to play them. Fortunately, providing these different file formats is easy to do via the HTML5 audio and source elements.

In addition, legacy browsers, such as Internet Explorer 8 and earlier, can also be supported via third-party plugins (such as Flash) as they were before. Gradually, legacy browsers will fade out of use, and the requirement to support them will cease to exist. But you can still guarantee their users access to your audio.

The examples in this chapter cover a wide range of real-life scenarios that you may encounter when adding audio to your web documents. However, they are by no means exhaustive. And although all the code used in the examples is available on the website, additional examples will be added in the future, so it's definitely worth checking them out.

Native audio is a major step forward in web technology and is matched at least by, and perhaps even surpassed by, video, which is the focus of the next chapter.

4

USING **VIDEO**

The popularity of video-sharing sites such as YouTube and Vimeo, combined with bandwidth speeds that makes online video feasible, have led to a huge demand for embedding video in web documents. Yet until recently the only way was by using third-party plugins such as Flash and QuickTime. HTML5 provides that missing standard method for embedding videos in web documents. Major browsers have begun to support it in their latest releases, so you can be confident that modern browsers can handle your video content.

This chapter covers the file formats and codecs supported by HTML5 video, how to convert between formats, and solutions to issues you might encounter. You'll also learn how to deliver video to browsers that don't support HTML5 video.

VIDEO CODECS AND FILE FORMATS

As with audio, HTML5 video has a number of different formats that you can use to encode video content in due to browser vendors being unable to agree on a standard. The video file formats available include Theora Ogg, MP4 (H.264), and WebM. Let's look at each in detail.

CODECS AND CONTAINERS

As mentioned in Chapter 3, a *codec* is a computer program that uses a compression algorithm to encode and/or decode a digital stream of data, making it more suitable for playback.

A *container* is a wrapper format whose specification describes how the different data elements within the container exist and interact together within a computer file.

THEORA OGG

Theora Ogg, as you've probably guessed, is also from the Xiph.Org Foundation (www.xiph.org). Like its audio counterpart, Theora Ogg is free and open, and has no licensing or royalty issues.

As with audio, Ogg is the name of the container format, and in this case Theora refers to the video-compression format that it uses. Earlier versions of the Theora codec showed it to be inferior to other similar codecs at the time, but it has improved a great deal and is now considered comparable to YouTube's H.264 output (before YouTube started encoding high-definition video).

Theora Ogg uses the `application/ogg` MIME type and the `video/ogg` video attribute type.

MP4 (H.264)

MPEG-4 Part 10, or MP4, is a compressed video format, which like the MP3 audio format (see Chapter 3) was defined by the Moving Picture Experts Group (MPEG; www.mpeg.org). It was developed to deliver DVD-quality video and audio in a small package. This small file size makes MP4 files highly suitable for portable players, and naturally, the web.

H.264 has been split into 17 different "profiles"; each of which provides additional features that usually increase the file size. Some are suitable for use with HTML5 video, whereas others are not. The Baseline and Main profiles are usually used for HTML5 video. For a full list of these profiles, see en.wikipedia.org/wiki/H.264#Profiles.

MP4 uses the video/mpeg MIME type and the video/mp4 video attribute type.

WEBM

WebM is a project (www.webmproject.org) that is supported by web-industry giants, such as Mozilla, Opera, Adobe, and Google. The aim of the project is to produce a high-quality, royalty-free, open video format.

The video content is compressed with the VP8 codec, which was developed by On2 Technologies (the company was acquired by Google in February 2010). The codec tends to be used within the WebM container.

WebM uses the video/webm MIME type and the video/webm video attribute type.

BROWSER SUPPORT FOR VIDEO FORMATS

When the first draft of the HTML5 specification was released, it recommended that browsers should support the Theora Ogg video format. Knowing that all browsers that supported HTML5 video would support a standard video format would have allowed you to guarantee availability of your video content to users when you served up a Theora Ogg video file. However, note the use of the phrase "would have."

Unfortunately, like the audio specification, both Nokia and Apple objected to the requirement to support Theora Ogg, which they regarded as not being widely supported and not as open and free as the Xiph.Org Foundation claimed. So the requirement was removed. As a result, you're back to having to supply your video content in more than one format to guarantee coverage of all browsers that support HTML5 video.

Table 4.1 contains a list of which vendors support certain video formats in their browsers.

TABLE 4.1 Video Formats and Browser Support

FORMAT	BROWSER				
Theora Ogg	Firefox 3.5+	Chrome 5+	Opera 10.5+		
MP4/H.264	Safari 3+	Chrome 5–?	IE9+	iOS	Android 2+
WebM	Firefox 4+	Chrome 6+	Opera 11+	IE9+	Android 2.3+

NOTE: Chrome currently supports MP4/H.264 but will drop support for it soon. Internet Explorer 9 will support WebM as long as a third-party plugin that can play it is installed.

In fact, you need to serve up at least two different formats, MP4 and WebM, in order to support the latest versions of the major browsers. This isn't too much of a chore if you're only serving up a few videos, because it can be easily done using the video and source elements mentioned in Chapter 2. For video-intensive sites, it can unfortunately be a burden because many files need to exist in at least two different formats, thus doubling the storage space required.

Because you'll have your video file in one format, the easiest way of providing the two formats is by converting from one format to the other.

Let's take a quick look at how you'd convert your video content between the different formats before diving into the code examples.

ENCODING YOUR VIDEO FILES

You might already have the video content that you want to display on your web document, or you might still need to record it. Let's assume that you already have the content, and that it is in one of the aforementioned formats, although it could just as easily not be. Either way it's not a problem because there are plenty of encoders on the market that you can use to convert your video content from one format to another.

TIP: It's wise to support at least MP4 and WebM to cover the latest versions of the major browsers. Safari supports MP4; Firefox and Opera support WebM; and Chrome and Internet Explorer 9 currently support both MP4 and WebM, although Chrome will drop support for MP4 in the near future and IE9 needs a plugin for WebM. However, you might also choose to support Theora Ogg, because WebM wasn't supported by Firefox until version 4, and Firefox doesn't support MP4 at all.

Here are three of my favourite encoders:

- **Miro Video Converter** (http://www.mirovideoconverter.com). As well as converting between audio formats, this converter also supports conversion of video files to Theora Ogg, MP4, and WebM. It really is all you need and runs on both Windows and Mac.

- **Handbrake** (http://handbrake.fr). This open source converter allows you to convert video files to MP4 and the Theora Ogg format. It runs on Windows, Mac, and Linux.

- **Media Converter** (http://www.mediaconverter.org). This online conversion application allows you to upload a file for conversion or provide the URL of an existing file. It allows you to convert files to Theora Ogg, MP4, and Flash FLV, among others.

Although you can choose from many other encoders, these are three solid encoders that you can use to get started.

MP4 ENCODING AND DELAYED PLAYBACK

Sometimes the way an MP4 file is coded can cause problems with its playback. Namely, the file doesn't start playing until it has downloaded completely. This is due to the encoding process placing the file index—with all the metadata on file length and so on—at the end of the file rather than the beginning.

If you find this is happening to your MP4 files, you can fix the problem by running the files through the QTIndexSwapper (http://renaun.com/blog/code/qtindexswapper) by Renaun Erickson of Adobe. QTIndexSwapper simply moves the index to the beginning of the file.

Now that you've converted your files, you're ready to start using them within your documents!

USING THE VIDEO ELEMENTS

Let's begin with some basic examples of embedding video files within a web document. You'll have previously encountered all the elements and attributes used in the examples in Chapter 2, so nothing should be new to you.

PLAYING A VIDEO FILE

The easiest example of them all is to play a simple video file of one format with default media controls for the user.

To play a WebM file, you use:

```
<video src="snowy-tree.webm" controls></video>
```

The control attribute informs the browser that it should display a set of basic video controls on top of the video player.

If you wanted the video to start playing as soon as the page loads, you could simply add the autoplay attribute:

```
<video src="snowy-tree.webm" controls autoplay></video>
```

You might also want the video to start playing immediately and then keep playing in a loop via the loop attribute:

```
<video src="snowy-tree.webm" controls autoplay loop></video>
```

It is, however, strongly advised not to do this: Not only is it annoying, but it can be an accessibility nightmare because a looping video file might play over added audio that's inserted for accessibility reasons.

You could also mute the video file on startup by using the muted attribute. Of course, if your video has no sound, this has no effect:

```
<video src="snowy-tree.webm" controls autoplay muted></video>
```

NOTES: None of the major browsers currently support the muted attribute. However, you can set it via the Media JavaScript API, which is discussed in Chapter 5.

All of the examples in this section and more can be found on the accompanying website at www.html5multimedia.com.

FIGURE 4.1 Restoring the browser's default media controls via the browser menu in Firefox 5.

By default, the browser will start loading the entire video file when the page loads. If you would prefer that the browser not do this (perhaps you think it's unlikely that users will want to view the video and don't want to waste bandwidth because they might be viewing your site over a mobile network), you can use the preload attribute and set it to none:

```
<video src="snowy-tree.webm" controls preload="none"></video>
```

You can also request that the browser load the video's metadata (e.g., file length) by setting the preload attribute to metadata:

```
<video src="snowy-tree.webm" controls preload="metadata"></video>
```

Any setting of the preload attribute merely suggests to the browser what your intentions are, but ultimately, the browser will decide what to do. The browser may, for example, ignore your suggestion due to a user setting in the browser.

If you want to hardcode the width and height of the video rather than letting the browser automatically decide for you, you can do so via the width and height attributes:

```
<video src="snowy-tree.webm" controls width="300" height="210">
→ </video>
```

You can also remove the controls entirely by omitting the controls attribute:

```
<video src="snowy-tree.webm"></video>
```

Note that the user can restore the default controls in most browsers by right-clicking on the video and selecting the controls from the displayed drop-down menu **Figure 4.1.**

TIP: If you also specify autoplay, the preload setting will be overridden because the video must be downloaded for it to play!

All of the preceding examples use just one video file format. But because you'll need to serve up more than one video file format to cover all major browsers, let's take a look at how to do that next.

PLAYING A VIDEO FILE WITH DIFFERENT SOURCES

Presenting different video file formats to the browser is quite easy using the source element, which you also used in the audio examples in Chapter 3.

Here is the code you need to provide two different sources for the video to play:

```
<video controls>
    <source src="snowy-tree.mp4" type="video/mp4">
    <source src="snowy-tree.webm" type="video/webm">
</video>
```

But let's also support Theora Ogg, just in case a Firefox 3.5 or Opera 10.5 user wants to view your video:

```
<video controls>
    <source src="snowy-tree.ogv" type="video/ogg">
    <source src="snowy-tree.mp4" type="video/mp4">
    <source src="snowy-tree.webm" type="video/webm">
</video>
```

NOTE: You probably won't need to add support for Theora Ogg, and you should only really bother if you know that you need to support specific older versions of Firefox.

The examples in the previous section, "Playing a Video File," where different attributes were applied to show you how they work and what they do, also apply to any video element that contains multiple source elements.

THE **type ATTRIBUTE**

When you use the source element within the video element, you'll notice that the type attribute moves from the video element to the source element. The reason is that the whole idea of serving up different sources is because they use different formats, and each source element needs to specify the format the source is in via its own type attribute.

The type attribute can also contain the actual codec that the video file is encoded in. For example:

```
<source src="snowy-tree.mp4" type='video/ogg; codecs="theora, vorbis"'>
<source src="snowy-tree.mp4" type='video/webm; codecs="vp8, vorbis"'>
<source src="snowy-tree.mp4" type='video/mp4; codecs="mp4a.40.2"'>
```

Including the codec in the type attribute can be beneficial because it helps the browser decide if it can play the file or not. It's best to only include the codec if you know for certain which codec was used to encode your video content.

Should you decide to include the codec, be *very careful* and ensure that you format the string correctly, paying particular attention to the quotes used; otherwise, the browser won't recognise the source.

In the preceding example, note how the entire string is enclosed within single quotes, the type and codecs attributes are separated by a semicolon, and the codecs values are contained within a double quote.

If you want to autoplay and loop your video, you would add the autoplay and loop attributes to the video element like this:

```
<video controls autoplay loop>
    <source src="snowy-tree.mp4" type="video/mp4">
    <source src="snowy-tree.webm" type="video/webm">
</video>
```

You can of course also autoplay and remove the controls like this:

```
<video autoplay>
    <source src="snowy-tree.mp4" type="video/mp4">
    <source src="snowy-tree.webm" type="video/webm">
</video>
```

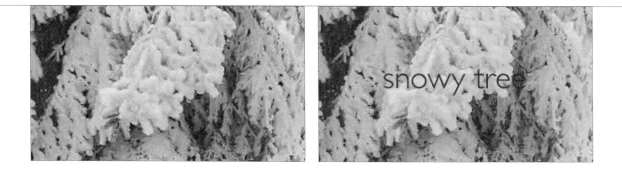

Notice that when autoplay is off, the first still from the video is displayed in the browser as an image. You might want to use a different image if the first still from the video isn't what you want to display; it might be blank or just not the still you want to show first.

If you want to use a different image, you can use the poster attribute to point at an image file to use instead:

```
<video controls poster="snowy-tree-poster.gif" width="300"
 → height="210">
    <source src="snowy-tree.mp4" type="video/mp4">
    <source src="snowy-tree.webm" type="video/webm">
</video>
```

You can get an idea of how the poster attribute works in **Figure 4.2**.

Now that you know how to play video files, you might want to think about the legacy browser fallback. How do you show video in legacy browsers? Let's take a look.

FIGURE 4.2 The image on the left displays the first still from the video that the browser shows by default; on the right, the same video is shown but with a defined poster image displayed instead.

PLAYING A VIDEO FILE WITH DIFFERENT
SOURCES AND LEGACY FALLBACK

Throughout this chapter I've recommended providing a fallback for legacy browsers, such as Internet Explorer 6 to 8, that don't support HTML5 and native multimedia. This of course means reverting to an old third-party plugin that these browsers understand, such as Flash.

Because browsers ignore what they don't understand, legacy browsers will ignore the video and source elements, and act as if they don't exist. This of course allows you to provide a simple link to the video file so it can be downloaded:

```
<video controls autoplay>

    <source src="snowy-tree.mp4" type="video/mp4">

    <source src="snowy-tree.webm" type="video/webm">

    <a href="snowy-tree.mp4">Download the video: snowy-tree.mp4</a>

</video>
```

You might prefer to actually provide an image link rather than a simple text link:

```
<video controls autoplay>

    <source src="snowy-tree.mp4" type="video/mp4">

    <source src="snowy-tree.webm" type="video/webm">

    <figure>

        <a href="snowy-tree.mp4">

            <img src="snowy-tree.gif" alt="Branches of a fern tree
            → covered in snow" height="210" width="300" />

            <figcaption>Download the video: snowy-tree.mp4
            → </figcaption>

        </a>

    </figure>

</video>
```

FIGURE 4.3 This is how the image and link to download the MP4 file might be displayed in Internet Explorer 8.

Download the video: snowy-tree.mp4

Figure 4.3 shows how this might look in Internet Explorer.

If you decide to support Flash and allow non-HTML5 browsers to play your video via Flash, you can of course do so using either the embed or object elements. You can then play the video using a downloaded Flash player (which you have uploaded to your server) and the object element.

You can also take advantage of the fact that Flash can play MP4 files, so there's no need to create another file in a different format. The following code shows how a Flash fallback can be achieved:

```
<video controls autoplay>
    <source src="snowy-tree.mp4" type="video/mp4">
    <source src="snowy-tree.webm" type="video/webm">
    <object type="application/x-shockwave-flash"
        data="player.swf?videoUrl=snowy-tree.mp4&autoPlay=true"
        height="210" width="300">
        <param name="movie"
        value="player.swf?videoUrl=snowy-tree.mp4&autoPlay=true">
    </object>
</video>
```

A non-HTML5 browser will ignore the two source elements because it doesn't know what to do with them. It will then recognise the object element, and provided Flash is installed, will play the video through the Flash player.

The same code using the embed element looks like this:

```
<video controls autoplay>
    <source src="snowy-tree.mp4" type="video/mp4">
    <source src="snowy-tree.webm" type="video/webm">
    <embed type="application/x-shockwave-flash" wmode="transparent"
        src="player.swf?videoUrl=snowy-tree.mp4&autoPlay=true"
        height="210" width="300">
</video>
```

It's better practice to use object instead of embed, because any content in the object start and end tags will be rendered even if the browser doesn't support the plugin that the object element specifies in its type attribute. This allows you to specify yet another fallback should you need to. As you can see in the previous object example, the param element will be read by browsers that don't understand the value specified by the type attribute in the object element.

Of course, you still need to rely on the fact that users have the Flash player installed on their computers, but this may not always be the case. Therefore, you can also add the image download link mentioned earlier as a final fallback, just in case Flash isn't installed:

```
<video controls autoplay>
    <source src="snowy-tree.mp4" type="video/mp4">
    <source src="snowy-tree.webm" type="video/webm">
    <object type="application/x-shockwave-flash"
        data="player.swf?videoUrl=snowy-tree.mp4&autoPlay=true"
        height="210" width="300">
        <param name="movie"
        value="player.swf?videoUrl=snowy-tree.mp4&autoPlay=true">
    </object>
    <a href="snowy-tree.mp4">Download the video: snowy-tree.mp4</a>
</video>
```

The download link here isn't a true fallback in the sense that if the browser falls back to Flash, the download link will also be displayed, but that's not necessarily a bad thing because it just provides another way to access the file.

There's plenty to think about when deciding which browsers you want to support and which fallbacks you want to provide to do so. Whatever you decide on, HTML5 multimedia should enable you to get the job done.

VIDEO FOR **EVERYBODY!**

You can read an excellent article by Kroc Camen of Camen Design (http://camendesign.com) on how to make video available to all without using JavaScript or browser sniffing. Kroc's site is definitely worth checking out for future reading because he keeps it up to date with any new developments or discoveries that he or others make.

You'll find the article at http://camendesign.com/code/video_for_everybody.

Of course, these days it isn't just modern and legacy desktop browsers that you need to worry about supporting. You also need to make your content available to users of modern mobiles, tablets, and other alternative browsing devices with video-playing capabilities. To optimise your web content for such devices, you also need to learn about *media types* and *media queries*, which is what you'll look at next.

TARGETING DEVICES WITH DIFFERENT VIDEO FILES USING MEDIA TYPES AND QUERIES

Let's say you wanted to serve up a different video file depending on the browser's capabilities and size. For example, you might want to play a smaller video, in both dimensions and file size, to a mobile phone that will have a small screen and possibly be retrieving data over a 3G connection. Is this even possible? It is if you use a combination of *media types* and *media queries*, and the media attribute in the source element.

Media types were introduced in CSS2 (www.w3.org/TR/CSS2/media.html) to enable you to target different devices with specific styling and/or style sheets. **Table 4.2** (on the next page) lists the media types.

TABLE 4.2 Media Types

TYPE	DEFINITION
all	Suitable for all devices.
braille	Aimed at Braille tactile feedback devices.
embossed	Aimed at paged braille printers.
handheld	Intended for handheld devices, such as mobile phones.
print	Targets paged material and material for display in print preview mode.
projection	Suitable for projected presentations.
screen	Suitable for displaying on a colour computer screen.
speech	Intended for speech synthesisers.
tty	Aimed at devices with a fixed-pitch character grid, such as a terminal.
tv	Intended for a television-type device.

You may have come across some of the media types listed in Table 4.2 before, although most of them are probably alien to you. If you've ever created a style sheet for printing content, you'll be familiar with the print media type; if you've ever attempted to target a mobile phone, the handheld type will also be familiar to you.

But it is the handheld type that has caused particular issues as technology has moved on. Initially, phones didn't have browsers that were capable of rendering HTML sites, so developers largely ignored them. When phones became "smarter" and came with improved browsers, the handheld media type wasn't being used in websites. Vendors then chose to ignore it and default to the screen media type instead. But something was needed to help combat this because website configurations that were meant for full-screen browsers were now rendering on phones, causing many an annoying scroll bar. This is where media queries come in.

Media queries were created by the W3C and have a complete specification of their own (see www.w3.org/TR/css3-mediaqueries). They are an extension to CSS3 media types that allow you to check for conditions of particular media features, such as width, height, and orientation, to deliver either different content or styling. You can check for a number of device features, the list of which appears in **Table 4.3**.

TABLE 4.3 Media Query Device Features

FEATURE	MIN/MAX PREFIXES	DEFINITION
width	Yes	The width of the target display area.
height	Yes	The height of the target display area.
device-width	Yes	The width of the device's rendering area.
device-height	Yes	The height of the device's rendering area.
orientation	Yes	Orientation of the rendering device: portait or landscape.
aspect-ratio	Yes	Ratio of target width to the height.
device-aspect-ratio	Yes	Ratio of device-width to the device-height.
resolution	Yes	Density of pixels in the device.
color	Yes	Number of bits per colour component.
color-index	Yes	Number of entries in colour lookup table.
grid	No	Tests if the device is grid-based or not.
monochrome	Yes	Number of bits per pixel in monochrome device.
scan	No	For TV browsing: progressive or scan.

The great thing is that you can combine media types and media queries to target certain devices using the *and* keyword:

```
screen and (min-device-width:300px)
```

You can also target all devices that don't match particular settings by using the logical *not* operator keyword:

```
not screen and (max-width:800px)
```

The *only* keyword can also be used to hide the settings from older browsers:

```
only screen and (max-width:800px)
```

Of course, these settings don't work on their own and need to be assigned to the `media` attribute of the required `source` element within the `video` container:

```
<source src="myVideo.webm" media=" screen and
→ (min-device-width:300px)">
```

The following code example serves a different video to all media types that have a maximum width of 600 pixels. Both WebM and MP4 formats are provided. Anything that doesn't match these features will move on to the succeeding source definitions:

```
<video controls>
    <source src="snowy-tree-small.mp4" type="video/mp4"
    → media="all and (max-width:600px)">

    <source src="snowy-tree-small.webm" type="video/webm"
    → media="all and (max-width:600px)">

    <source src="snowy-tree-medium.webm" type="video/webm">

    <source src="snowy-tree-medium.mp4" type="video/mp4">
</video>
```

If you want to also provide a medium-sized video file based on a larger maximum display width of 800 pixels, you can do so like this:

```
<video controls>
    <source src="snowy-tree-small.mp4" type="video/mp4"
    → media="screen and (max-width:600px)">

    <source src="snowy-tree-small.webm" type="video/webm"
    → media="screen and (max-width:600px)">

    <source src="snowy-tree-medium.webm" type="video/webm"
    → media="screen and (max-width:800px)">

    <source src="snowy-tree-medium.mp4" type="video/mp4"
    → media="screen and (max-width:800px)">

    <source src="snowy-tree-large.webm" type="video/webm">

    <source src="snowy-tree-large.mp4" type="video/mp4">
</video>
```

TESTING WITH MEDIA TYPES AND QUERIES

You might be wondering how on earth you would test media types and queries if you don't have specific devices available to you.

With the examples that I've provided, simply changing the size of the browser window and then refreshing the page will usually result in the desired outcome.

You can also use the ProtoFluid application (http://app.protofluid.com), which allows you to load a website (even those running on your local server) and change the view to that of a handful of phones (such as Blackberry and iPhone) and monitors of various sizes, among other devices.

You can see how the code in the section "Targeting Devices with Different Video Files Using Media Types and Queries" works in ProtoFluid in **Figure 4.4** and **Figure 4.5**.

Of course, nothing beats testing your code on the real thing, but that isn't always a viable option given the sheer number of devices on the market.

NOTE: Firefox completely ignores media queries, so changing the browser window size will have no effect. I suggest using Opera, which does exactly what it's supposed to.

FIGURE 4.4 Selecting the iPhone size in ProtoFluid displays the smaller video file.

FIGURE 4.5 Selecting the desktop 800×600 size in ProtoFluid displays the medium video file.

Again, any device that has a maximum display size that is larger than 600 pixels or 800 pixels will ignore the smaller sizes and play whichever one of the WebM or MP4 larger videos that it is capable of playing.

These are just some simple examples of what you might want to achieve when targeting different devices. By combining media types and queries, you can target any device to meet your specific requirements. Unfortunately, none of the previous examples discussed will work with Android.

ANDROID AND VIDEO

The implementation of HTML5 video in Android is nothing short of shockingly poor. For this reason, it deserves its own small section to prevent you from tearing your hair out.

Android supports MP4 files from version 2.0 and WebM from version 2.3.

You shouldn't use the type attribute with the video or source element when defining the video file you want Android to use. For some reason, this confuses Android and it ignores the source.

In addition, Android will completely ignore the controls attribute, and you'll have to either implement your own controls via the JavaScript API (which is the subject of Chapter 5), or to achieve autoplay, play the video via the API on page load.

Android also won't show the first frame of the video as an image; it instead displays a video icon. It does however recognise and understand the poster attribute, so if you specify an image with that attribute, it will display that image correctly.

The code for specifying a video for Android follows, along with the JavaScript required to play the video on Android when the user presses the video icon. I'll defer the explanation of this JavaScript for now but will discuss it in detail in Chapter 5:

TIP: Peter Gasston, a web developer and author of many articles and a book on CSS3, provides an in-depth tutorial on how to make HTML5 video work on Android phones. Be sure to check out what he has to say at www.broken-links.com/2010/07/08/making-html5-video-work-on-android-phones if you have problems working with HTML5 video on Android phones.

```html
<!DOCTYPE html>
<html>
<head>
    <title>Playing a Video File: Media Query Android</title>
    <script>
        function play() {
            var video = document.getElementById('video');
            video.addEventListener('click',function(){
                video.play();
            },false);
        }
    </script>
</head>
<body onload="play();">
    <video controls>
        <source src="snowy-tree-small.mp4" media="screen and
        →  (max-width:800px)">
        <source src="snowy-tree-large.mp4" type="video/mp4">
    </video>
</body>
</html>
```

The preceding issues mentioned only affect the default browser that comes with Android. If the user uses another mobile browser, such as Opera Mobile, the preceding code isn't necessary. It's a good bet that Google will improve Android's implementation of HTML5 video in a future release. And by the time you read this, it may have already been updated.

WRAPPING **UP**

You should now be aware of just how easy it is to add video to your website using HTML5 native multimedia. You are probably also aware that there are still a number of details you need to consider before doing so. For example:

- Which browsers should you support?

- Will you support legacy browsers?

- Should you support mobile devices? If so, which ones?

These are just some of the questions you may need to ask before forging ahead. Once you've made those decisions, however, harnessing the power of HTML5 multimedia to deliver video to your users is relatively simple. With the standardised method of delivery the multimedia part of the HTML5 specification brings, you know which viewers you'll reach and what kind of experience they will have.

So far you've been leaving it up to the browser to provide the video (and audio) controls. And these controls vary from one browser to the next.

In the next chapter you'll learn how to use the HTML5 multimedia JavaScript APIs included as part of the HTML5 specification to create your own custom controls for both audio and video. Let's go!

5

JAVASCRIPT API AND **CUSTOM** **CONTROLS**

HTML5 audio and video provide a lot of functionality out of the box, but it doesn't stop there. HTML5 also provides a wonderfully easy-to-use Media JavaScript API that you can use to extend that basic functionality in other ways.

You've all seen the default controls that browsers add to your video or audio content, and some are pretty ugly. Well, an excellent use of the JavaScript API is to roll out your own multimedia controls. You can style them however you like using CSS, and then hook them up via the API to control your video and audio.

This chapter describes the attributes, methods, and events of the JavaScript API and then shows you how to put together your own control set and connect it to make it functional.

Let's take control!

WHAT IS JAVASCRIPT?

JavaScript is a commonly used client-side scripting language that you can use to provide extra functionality to a website. Because the code is client side, it is part of the HTML page and it's up to the browser to do something with it. Therefore, having the Media API as part of the HTML5 specification ensures a standard implementation of the API across browsers.

The Media API discussed here is a JavaScript API, and it is assumed that you have an understanding of this language. If you don't, I recommend the JavaScript tutorial at www.quirksmode.org/js/intro.html. It will give you a good introduction to the JavaScript language, which will aid you with your understanding of the contents of this chapter.

When you've finished the tutorial, or if you are already familiar with JavaScript, read on!

EXPLORING THE API ATTRIBUTES

It's important for you to know about the attributes that each multimedia element can have as part of the JavaScript API. Each attribute along with its description is listed in **Table 5.1**.

Some attributes are specific to video only; these are listed in **Table 5.2**.

For those attributes that raise an event when their value is changed, the event name is given for easy reference. See the section "Harnessing the API Events" later in this chapter for a list of events.

TABLE 5.1 Audio and Video Attributes

ATTRIBUTE	DESCRIPTION
duration	Contains the duration of the audio or video. This is a read-only attribute and may only be available if the video has been preloaded. When this value becomes available for reading, the durationchange event is raised.
volume	Contains the volume setting for the audio or video. 0 is the lowest value; 1.0 is the highest. When this value is changed, the volumechanged event is raised.
paused	Is a boolean attribute that indicates whether or not the audio or video resource is currently paused. When this value changes to true, a pause event is raised. When this value changes to false, a play event is raised.
playbackRate	Indicates the required speed at which the audio or video resource is to be played. Valid values range from –1.0 to 1.0. A negative value plays the resource backwards faster; a positive value plays it forward faster. A value of 0 stops playback. When this value changes, a ratechange event is raised.
ended	Is a boolean attribute that indicates whether the audio or video resource has finished playing (and the play direction is forward! See defaultPlaybackRate later in this table and playbackRate earlier).
autoplay	Is a boolean attribute that indicates whether or not the audio or video is to play automatically.

TABLE 5.1 Audio and Video Attributes *(continued)*

ATTRIBUTE	DESCRIPTION
loop	Is a boolean attribute that indicates whether or not the audio or video resource is set to loop.
controls	Is a boolean attribute that indicates whether or not the browser is to display its default control set on the audio or video.
muted	Is a boolean attribute that indicates whether or not the audio or video is muted.
src	Contains the URL to the media source as set in the attribute of the audio or video element.
currentSrc	Initially empty, this contains the URL to the media source that's actually selected for play by the audio or video element, usually set via a child source element.
startTime	Contains the start-time value of the audio or video element. This is usually 0 but can occasionally be a positive value for various reasons, such as being part of a live stream or if it's a fragment from a larger audio or video resource.
crossOrigin	Contains the setting for the audio or video element's crossOrigin attribute. This is intended to allow or prohibit cross-origin media of the audio source using the CORS (Cross-Origin Resource Sharing) specification (see Chapter 2 for more details).
networkState	Contains the current network state of the audio or video element.
	It can have one of four settings (the numeric value is provided in brackets after the setting name):
	• NETWORK_EMPTY (0) — Indicates that the element has not yet been initialised.
	When this value is set, the emptied event is raised. The abort and error events can also be raised when this value is set.
	• NETWORK_IDLE (1) — A resource to play has been selected but is not currently being played.
	When this value is set, the suspend event is raised. The abort and error events can also be raised.
	• NETWORK_LOADING (2) — The browser is currently attempting to download data.
	When this value is set, the following events are raised: loadstart, progress, and stalled.
	• NETWORK_NO_SOURCE (3) — The element is currently looking for a resource to play but hasn't yet found one.

TABLE 5.1 Audio and Video Attributes *(continued)*

ATTRIBUTE	DESCRIPTION
preload	Contains the value of the element's `preload` attribute, which is used to provide a hint to the browser on how the media source is to be preloaded (see Chapter 2 for more details).
buffered	Contains the time range of the `audio` or `video` element that the browser has currently buffered (if any). This returns a `TimeRange` object.
readyState	Contains the current ready state of the `audio` or `video` element and can contain one of five possible values (the numeric value is provided in brackets after the value name):

	• HAVE_NOTHING (0)	There is currently no information on the element available.
	• HAVE_METADATA (1)	The metadata of the element in question is currently available. In the case of the `video` element, it also indicates that the video's dimensions are available. The resource's start position is currently unknown.
		When this value is set, the `loadedmetadata` event is raised.
	• HAVE_CURRENT_DATA (2)	Enough data has been retrieved to know the start position of the audio or video but not enough to actually play it.
		When this value is set, the `loadeddata` event is raised.
	• HAVE_FUTURE_DATA (3)	Enough data has been retrieved so that the resource can be played. Playing the resource now, however, might mean that playback may attempt to overtake the amount of the resource retrieved.
		When this value is set, the `canplay` event is raised.
	• HAVE_ENOUGH_DATA (4)	Enough of the data has been retrieved that the resource can be played without fear of playback reaching the end of the available data before the end of the resource has been loaded.
		When this value is set, the `canplaythrough` event is raised.

You could check this attribute periodically to see when to start/stop displaying a waiting icon for example.

seeking	Is a boolean attribute that indicates whether the browser is currently looking for a different playback position within the audio or video resource. For example, the user may have dragged the default controls forward to play at a later point in the resource.

TABLE 5.1 Audio and Video Attributes *(continued)*

ATTRIBUTE	DESCRIPTION
currentTime	Contains the current time in seconds that the playback position within the audio or video resource has reached. When this value changes, the timeupdate event is raised. When this value equals the end of the media resource, the ended event is raised.
initialTime	Contains the initial playback position of the audio or video resource.
startOffsetTime	Contains a Date object representing the current timeline offset (the explicit date and time corresponding to the zero time in the resource) within the resource.
defaultPlaybackRate	Indicates the required speed at which the audio or video resource is to be played when it starts. Valid values range from -1.0 to 1.0. A negative value plays the resource backwards faster; a positive value plays it forward faster. A value of 0 stops playback. Normal play rate is 0.1. When this value changes, a ratechange event is raised.
played	Returns a TimeRanges object indicating the time ranges, if any, that the browser has so far played of the resource.
seekable	Returns a TimeRanges object that indicates the time ranges, if any, of the media resource that the browser can "seek" to (i.e., look ahead), which depends on how much of the resource is actually loaded.
mediaGroup	Contains the resource's mediaGroup attribute value, which allows multiple media elements to be linked together via a common name/group (see Chapter 2 for more details), if set.
controller	Contains the resource's current media controller, if set; otherwise null.
defaultMuted	Is a boolean that reflects the value of the resource's muted attribute (see Chapter 2).
audioTracks	Contains the live audio track list that is available in the media element's resource, if any.
videoTracks	Contains the live video track list that is available in the media element's resource, if any.
textTracks	Is a read-only attribute that contains a list of the text tracks available in the media element's resource, if any.

THE **TIMERANGE** OBJECT

Some of the attributes mentioned in Table 5.1 return a TimeRange object, which essentially contains the following bits of data:

- **length.** The number of ranges actually in the object.

- **start(index).** The timestamp of the start time of the range for the given index.

- **end(index).** The timestamp of the end time of the range for the given index.

Thus, if a particular TimeRange object's length is 1, you can access the start and end timestamps of that particular object via start(0) and end(0), respectively.

TABLE 5.2 Video Attributes

ATTRIBUTE	DESCRIPTION
width	Contains the width of the video element in pixels or percentage. Altering this value will not affect the value of videoWidth.
height	Contains the height of the video element in pixels or percentage. Altering this value will not affect the value of videoHeight.
videoWidth	Is a read-only attribute that contains the actual width of the video media file in pixels, or 0 if it's not known, at the time the video is loaded.
videoHeight	Is a read-only attribute that contains the actual height of the video media file in pixels, or 0 if it's not known, at the time the video is loaded.
poster	Contains the URL to the poster image for the video, if any.

Phew, that's quite a list of attributes! But don't worry; many of them you might not ever use. I've made an attempt at putting them in order of those you might be most interested in.

Let's look at a couple of quick examples that show how you might use these attributes. If, for example, you wanted to grab the current played time position of the video, you'd use the currentTime attribute:

```
<script>
    var video = document.getElementsByTagName("video")[0];
    alert(video.currentTime);
</script>
```

You grab a handle to the video object using the standard getElementsByTagName() JavaScript function (there's only one video here, and you know that, hence the index of 0), and then read the video's currentTime attribute. This could of course be 0 if the video hasn't started yet and is constantly updated as the video plays.

Another example would be to check if the video is looping, and if so, stop it from doing so:

```
<script>
    var video = document.getElementsByTagName("video")[0];
    if (video.loop) video.loop = false;
</script>
```

As you can see, you can achieve this by checking if the loop attribute is true, and if so, setting it to false to stop the video from looping.

These are just two brief examples of how you can use the attributes. You'll see plenty more examples when you start putting together your own media controls later in this chapter.

Tables 5.1 and 5.2 contain the entire list of attributes just in case you want to try one or more in the future and are curious as to what does what and where. Also, you might have noticed that changing some of these attributes raises events that you can catch, allowing you to act on them.

Let's take a closer look at these events.

Because JavaScript adds interactivity to web documents, when a user performs an action, there needs to be a way of detecting that the action occurred. This is the role of events.

A number of events in the Media JavaScript API can be raised based on value changes, method calls, and browser actions. Listening to certain events and responding to them can be key when rolling out your own control set for audio and video resources.

A full list of the events that can be raised is provided in **Table 5.3**.

TIP: If JavaScript events are new to you, check out www.quirksmode.org/js/introevents.html for a good solid introduction.

TABLE 5.3 Events Raised in the Media JavaScript API

EVENT	DESCRIPTION
loadstart	Is raised when the browser starts looking for media data to load.
progress	Is raised when the browser is retrieving media data.
suspend	Is raised when the browser was fetching media data but paused and has not yet fetched the entire media resource.
abort	Is raised when the browser stops fetching media data but not because of an error.
error	Is raised when an error occurred while the browser was fetching the media data.
emptied	Is raised when the network connection was lost while the browser was fetching media data or the load() method was called when one such method was already in progress.
stalled	Is raised when the browser is attempting to fetch media data, but for some reason the data isn't being transferred.
loadedmetadata	Is raised when the duration and dimensions of the media resource have been acquired by the browser.
loadeddata	Is raised when the browser knows the start position of the media resource.
canplay	Is raised when the browser can start playback for the first time but can't guarantee that if playback begins now that it won't have to pause to fetch more media data.

TABLE 5.3 Events Raised in the Media JavaScript API *(continued)*

EVENT	DESCRIPTION
canplaythrough	Is raised when the browser is capable of playing the media resource from start to finish without having to pause to fetch more media data.
playing	Is raised when playback of a media resource is ready to start after having been previously paused or delayed due to lack of sufficient media data.
waiting	Is raised when the browser has stopped playback due to insufficient media data being available. It does, however, expect the required data to become available shortly.
seeking	Is raised when the media resource's seeking attribute is set to true.
seeked	Is raised when the media resource's seeking attribute is set to false.
ended	Is raised when the media resource stops playing because it has finished.
durationchange	Is raised when the media resource's duration attribute has been updated.
timeupdate	Is raised when the media resource's current playback position has been changed (e.g., as part of normal playback).
play	Is raised when the media resource that was previously paused no longer is paused, and normal playback has resumed.
pause	Is raised after the pause() method has returned and the media resource has been paused.
ratechange	Is raised when either the media resource's defaultPlaybackRate or playbackRate attributes are changed.
volumechange	Is raised when the media resource's volume or muted attribute has changed.

Events can be quite useful when you want to react to various media resource attributes and states being changed, even if it's only to update an onscreen display.

Let's reuse one of the earlier short examples. If you wanted to grab and display the current time of the video as it's playing, you'd naturally want to update the time as it changes. To do this, you'd listen for the timechange event and then act on it:

```
<div id="time">0</div>
<script>
    var video = document.getElementsByTagName("video")[0];
    video.addEventListener('timechange', function() {
        document.getElementById("time").innerHTML =
        → video.currentTime;
    }, false);
</script>
```

This code adds an event listener (more on this later) for the timechange event. When it is raised, it updates the time div with the current video played time. Because the timechange event is raised as the video's currentTime attribute is changed, this code will keep the display updated.

You'll use a video in the examples throughout the rest of the chapter (unless otherwise mentioned). Although nearly all the attributes, events, and methods apply to both audio and video, a video example helps to visualise them better.

As the video is playing, you'll need to move or give the impression of movement within a progress bar. Simply reacting to the timeupdate event can facilitate that task, because you can easily read the currentTime attribute and work out the percentage of the video played. You'll revisit progress bars later in the chapter when you learn how to create one.

But before you start looking at code and how you actually use the API, you need to know about methods.

USING THE API METHODS

Methods are small subroutines that tell an object, in this case an audio or video object, what to do. You don't need to know the ins and outs of what a particular method does internally. You just need to know that it exists, can be called, what it does, and the expected outcome.

The Media JavaScript API contains a handful of methods that are all aptly named and do exactly what they say they do (**Table 5.4**).

It's not a long list of methods for sure, but enough to be able to create your own simple set of media controls and use it to manipulate your audio and video media.

If you wanted to play the video when a certain button is clicked (which you will of course when implementing your own media controls!), you could do the following:

```
<button id="play" title="play" onclick="playVideo()">play</button>
<script>
    function playVideo() {
        var video = document.getElementsByTagName("video")[0];
        video.play();
    }
</script>
```

This code defines a simple HTML button and specifies that the playVideo() JavaScript function should be called when the button is clicked. The playVideo() function simply calls the video's play() method, which starts the video playing!

TIP: You may have noticed that there is no stop() method. Well, stopping the playback is pretty much the same as pausing it. The only difference is that you'd probably also want to set the media resource's currentTime attribute to the start of the media resource, which is 0.

By now you're absolutely bored to the back teeth with looking at lists of attributes, events, and methods. Well, as interesting and useful as they may be, so am I. So, let's move on to see just how useful they can be as you create a simple HTML5 video player with custom controls.

TABLE 5.4 Media API Methods

METHOD	DESCRIPTION
load()	Causes all activity on a media resource to be suspended immediately, and the element in question is reset to default values (for a comprehensive list of the default values that are set, go to www.whatwg.org/specs/web-apps/current-work/multipage/the-video-element. html#dom-media-load). This method causes the loadstart event to be raised.
play()	Informs the media element to begin playback of a media resource. If the media resource was previously paused, the resource's paused attribute will be set to false and the play event raised.
pause()	Causes a media resource to stop playing. This will cause the media element's paused attribute to be set to true and therefore raise a pause event.
canPlayType(type)	Takes a string representation of a MIME type (e.g., audio/ogg, video/mp4) as a parameter and returns a string value indicating the browser's perceived ability to play that particular media type. The values that can be returned include: • **An empty string** The browser is unable to play a media resource of this type. • **"maybe"** The browser can't say for certain that it can or cannot play a media resource of this type. • **"probably"** The browser is pretty sure it can play a media resource of this type.
addTextTrack(kind, [label],[language])	Returns and adds a text track, which it also adds to the media element's list of text tracks. The kind parameter can be one of: • subtitles • captions • descriptions • chapters • metadata The optional label and language parameters default to an empty string if they're not provided. You'll read more about text tracks in Chapter 8.

CREATING A SIMPLE VIDEO PLAYER WITH CUSTOM CONTROLS

While creating custom controls, you'll incorporate many of the elements you've learned about in previous chapters and in this one.

To begin, you'll need a video with sound. The previous video example of the snowy tree moving gently in the wind shows that I'm not very creative when it comes to choosing video. So, for this example, I've chosen grass blowing in the wind, complete with windy sounds and rustling grass—exciting stuff.

The basic HTML5 code for this little video setup is code that you've seen before and therefore isn't new to you:

```
<video controls>
    <source src="grass-in-the-wind-sma.mp4" type="video/mp4">
    <source src="grass-in-the-wind-sma.webm" type="video/webm">
</video>
```

Next, you'll add buttons to use as your Play/Pause and Stop buttons.

NOTES: The code for this simple video player example is available on the website at www.html5multimedia.com.

On some occasions there might be better or quicker ways to write the JavaScript functions. But the purpose of this code is to show you what you can achieve via the Media JavaScript API. Therefore, I think it's easier to see it explained via verbose JavaScript.

FIGURE 5.1 A boring video player.

ADDING PLAY/PAUSE AND STOP BUTTONS

Using simple HTML, again nothing you're not familiar with, you'll add the two buttons in a div below the video element definition:

```
<div id="controls">
    <button id="playpause" title="play">play</button>
    <button id="stop" title="stop">stop</button>
</div>
```

And there you have it; two simple, but currently useless, buttons that you can style however you like. For now, let's leave them as they are (**Figure 5.1**).

NOTE: You could of course use hyperlinks instead of buttons, but I have chosen to use buttons here.

You'll use the same button for playing and pausing the video because you'll only ever have one and not the other. Check out the browser's default media controls. When you click Play, it becomes a Pause button. You'll mimic that behaviour.

Notice that I've added a controls attribute to the video element. Why? I'm just playing it safe. Because you'll add all your custom controls using the JavaScript API, if users have JavaScript turned off, they won't have any controls. So you'll leave the controls attribute where it is and then remove it via JavaScript, which also won't happen if users have JavaScript turned off. Therefore, the attribute is no problem.

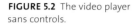

FIGURE 5.2 The video player sans controls.

Let's add the first piece of JavaScript and actually remove the default controls from the video:

```
<script>
    var video = document.getElementsByTagName("video")[0];
    video.controls = false;
</script>
```

You grab a handle to the video object using the standard getElementsByTagName() JavaScript function and then, using that handle, you set the boolean controls attribute to false. Your video player now looks like the one in **Figure 5.2**.

Next, you'll create a function for the buttons to call when they're actually clicked. Let's do the Stop button first, because it's the easiest.

You define the function stopVideo() and add it to the Stop button's onclick event:

```
function stopVideo() {
    video.pause();
    video.currentTime = 0;
}
<button id="stop" title="stop" onclick="stopVideo()">stop</button>
```

As mentioned earlier, stopping the video is pretty much the same as pausing it except you also reset the video's time to the beginning. As you can see, these tasks are achieved by calling the video's pause() method and then setting the currentTime attribute to 0.

The Play and Pause buttons naturally follow a similar pattern but are slightly more complex. You need to grab a handle to the button object because you'll need to make changes to it like this:

```
var ppbutton = document.getElementById("playpause");
```

You then define another function—for this example, call it togglePlay()—and assign it to the Play/Pause button:

```
function togglePlay() {
    if (video.paused || video.ended) {
        if (video.ended) video.currentTime = 0;
        ppbutton.title = "pause";
        ppbutton.innerHTML = "pause";
        video.play();
    }
    else {
        ppbutton.title = "play";
        ppbutton.innerHTML = "play";
        video.pause();
    }
}
<button id="playpause" title="play" onclick="togglePlay()">play
→ </button>
```

Let's look at the function more closely.

You first check if the video is currently in a paused or ended state. If it's ended, you reset the currentTime to 0 (much the same as you did in stopVideo()). Then you set the button's title attribute and text to "pause" and call the play() method to play the video.

If the video is not paused or ended, then obviously it's currently playing (and you want to pause it). So you change the button's title attribute and text to "play" and then call the pause() method to actually pause the video.

FIGURE 5.3 The custom video player with Play/Pause and Stop buttons.

As it is now, the video player changes the Play button to Pause when you click it and vice versa (**Figure 5.3**). The Play/Pause and Stop buttons now do exactly what they're supposed to.

You've made a good start on customising your controls. But what if users managed to play or pause the video without using your controls? How can they do that, you ask? Well, some browsers (e.g., Firefox) allow you to reinstate the controls by right-clicking on the video and choosing Show Controls. If a user clicks your Play button and then uses these default controls to pause the video, your controls look broken because the values shown on the Play/Pause buttons become out of sync with the actual state of the video. This where events come in.

LISTENING FOR EVENTS

As mentioned in Table 5.4, when the pause() and play() methods are called, they raise two events, pause and play, respectively. So all your code needs to do is listen for them and act accordingly.

To listen for an event, you use the addEventListener() method (which you saw briefly earlier) to call on the video object. So to listen for the pause and play events, you need to add this:

```
video.addEventListener('play', function() {
    /*...do stuff...*/
}, false);
video.addEventListener('pause', function() {
    /*...do stuff...*/
}, false);
```

And the "stuff" that you need to do in this case is simply to update the button's text accordingly, like this:

```
video.addEventListener('play', function() {
    ppbutton.title = "pause";
    ppbutton.innerHTML = "pause";
}, false);
video.addEventListener('pause', function() {
    ppbutton.title = "play";
    ppbutton.innerHTML = "play";
}, false);
```

Now if you use the browser's default controls to play/pause the video, your custom controls will still show the correct values.

Because you've now added the updating of the button values to the event listeners, you no longer need to do it in the togglePlay() function; it will now happen automatically when the event is raised. So togglePlay() now looks like this:

```
function togglePlay() {
    if (video.paused || video.ended) {
        if (video.ended) video.currentTime = 0;
        video.play();
    }
    else {
        video.pause();
    }
}
```

You also need to add an event listener for the ended event so you can correctly update the buttons when video playback ends normally. Do so like this:

```
video.addEventListener('ended', function() { this.pause(); }, false);
```

The `this` in question in the preceding line of code is the video, and calling `pause()` simply pauses the video, which in turn will raise the pause event. Then the Play/Pause button will be updated accordingly via the listener you've already added for the pause event.

This same logic applies for all the default controls that you will see on the browser, because your code will need to listen for all of them as well and act accordingly. You'll be adding event listeners and acting on them throughout the rest of the examples in this chapter.

Next, you need to control volume and mute.

ADDING VOLUME AND MUTE BUTTONS

As with the Play/Pause and Stop buttons, the principle of adding Volume and Mute buttons is the same:

- Add HTML buttons

- Create JavaScript functions to interact with the video via the API

- Add the JavaScript functions to the HTML button's `onclick` event

- Add appropriate events to catch the default control's behaviour (if required)

So once again you'll add new buttons—nothing fancy for the moment, just three simple buttons—one each for increasing and decreasing the volume, and also for muting/unmuting the sound:

```
<button id="volumeDown" title="-">-</button>
<button id="volumeUp" title="+">+</button>
<button id="mute" title="mute">mute</button>
```

NOTE: You could use the new HTML5 range element for the volume controls, which is ideal for functionality such as this. However, not all browsers currently support this element; Opera, Chrome, and Safari are the only ones that do. Hence, buttons are used in the example.

Now you need to define those functions, one for changing the volume and one for toggling the mute:

```
function changeVolume(direction) {
    var volume = Math.floor(video.volume * 10) / 10;
    video.muted = false;
    if (direction == "-") {
        if (volume <= 0.1) video.volume = 0;
        else video.volume -= 0.1;
    }
    else {
        if (volume >= 0.9) video.volume = 1;
        else video.volume += 0.1;
    }
}
```

Let's look at changeVolume() first.

You first grab the current volume setting of the video via the video's volume attribute, and then round it down to the nearest decimal place using JavaScript's Math.floor() function. Next, you set the video's muted attribute to "false" (you don't have to do this, but if someone's changing the volume, that person probably wants to unmute the video automatically if it's muted).

Then you check the direction parameter passed in by the button's call to changeVolume() to see if the volume should be decreased or increased. A "-" indicates a decrease, and a "+"indicates an increase. If it's a decrease, you check whether the current volume is already less than 0.1 (you decrease and increase the volume in steps of 0.1), and if so, you simply set the video's volume attribute to 0. Otherwise, you decrease the volume by 0.1. Almost the opposite occurs for an increase in volume; 1 is the highest value.

Now you define a function, toggleMute(), to toggle the mute status of the video:

```
function toggleMute() {
    var mute = document.getElementById("mute");
    if (video.muted) {
        mute.title = "mute";
        mute.innerHTML = "mute";
        video.muted = false;
    }
    else {
        mute.title = "unmute";
        mute.innerHTML = "unmute";
        video.muted = true;
    }
}
```

As you can see in the preceding code, you first need to get a reference to the mute button object so you can use it, because, as with the Play/Pause button, you need to change the text and value.

Then you check the video's muted attribute to see if it's already muted. If so, you change the button's value to "mute" and set the video's muted attribute to "false." Otherwise, you set the button's value and title to "unmute" and set the video's muted attribute to "true."

Now you need to add the functions to their appropriate button onclick events:

```
<button id="volumeDown" title="-" onclick="changeVolume('-')">-
→   </button>
<button id="volumeUp" title="+" onclick="changeVolume('+')">+
→   </button>
<button id="mute" title="mute" onclick="toggleMute()">mute</button>
```

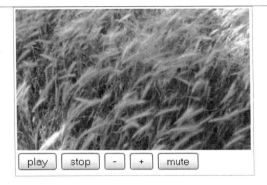

In this case you don't need to listen for any events unless you're updating a display of the player's current controls. If you did want to react to changes in volume, you could add a listener for the volumechange event, which is raised when either the volume or mute values are changed.

The buttons are finished. Your player now has three more working buttons (**Figure 5.4**), and they're fully functional.

Enough with the buttons for the moment. How can you show your users how much of the video they've seen? For that you need a progress bar.

ADDING A PROGRESS BAR

To add a progress bar, you again need to add the HTML for it first:

```
<div id="progressBar"><span id="played"></span></div>
```

NOTE: Ideally, the new HTML5 progress element would be used to add a progress bar. Unfortunately, it's currently only supported by Opera and Chrome, so a simple div and span combination is used instead.

FIGURE 5.5 The video player displays a progress bar that currently does nothing.

In addition, you also need to style it with a little bit of simple CSS to make it work visually:

```
#progressBar {
    border:1px solid #aaa;
    color:#fff;
    width:295px;
    height:20px;
}
#played {
    background-color:#aaa;
    height:20px;
    display:inline-block;
}
```

The width and heights are rather arbitrary, but that doesn't matter at this point because you can style the progress bar however you desire. With this code, you now have a crude progress bar (**Figure 5.5**).

Basically, what you'll do next is increase the percentage width of the played span within the progressBar div as the video is playing.

You define a function called updateProgress(), which you'll use to capture the video's currentTime setting and increase the width of the played span accordingly:

FIGURE 5.6 The video player and its working progress bar. Huzzah!

```
function updateProgress() {
    var value = 0;
    if (video.currentTime > 0) {
        value = Math.floor((100 / video.duration) *
        → video.currentTime);
    }
    document.getElementById("played").style.width = value + "%";
}
```

The function works out the percentage of the video played using the video's full duration compared to the currentTime (which is where within the video's full time it currently is).

Of course, to make the progress bar work, you need to listen for an event that tells you when currentTime has changed so you can call the updateProgress() function and actually update the progress bar—in this case, the timeupdate event:

```
video.addEventListener('timeupdate', updateProgress, false);
```

And that's it. Playing the video will raise the timeupdate event as it's playing, which in turn will call the updateProgress() function that will update the progress bar.

Your slightly better-than-average video player now has a working progress bar (**Figure 5.6**)!

To make this simple video player even more useful, why not add fast-forward and rewind buttons?

ADDING FAST-FORWARD AND REWIND BUTTONS

Yes, it's back to adding buttons I'm afraid. But you're a dab hand at adding them by now, so I won't need to tell you what to do until you get to the JavaScript stage.

Let's define the buttons and throw in the function names for the onclick events because you now know what's what:

```
<button id="rewind" title="reverse" onclick="changePlaybackSp
eed('-');" >&laquo;</button>
```

```
<button id="ffwd" title="fast forward" onclick="changePlaybackSp
eed('+');" >&raquo;</button>
```

You'll use the HTML entities « and » to mimic the typical symbols you find on such buttons: « and » respectively.

Notice that the name of the function you'll define is changePlaybackSpeed(). The attribute that you'll change to make this work is the playbackRate attribute that you encountered in Table 5.1.

There is a caveat though: Currently, only the WebKit-based browsers, Safari and Chrome, support the playbackRate attribute. Therefore, the only way you can sort of mimic the intended functionality on other browsers is to alter the video's currentTime attribute, moving it either forward or backwards:

```
function changePlaybackSpeed(direction) {
    if (video.playbackRate != undefined) {
        if (direction == "-") video.playbackRate -= 1;
        else video.playbackRate += 1;
    }
    else {
        if (direction == "-") video.currentTime -= 1;
        else video.currentTime += 1;
    }
}
```

FIGURE 5.7 Your fully functional but rather bland video player that could really do with a bit of CSS love.

FIGURE 5.8 A styled version of the video player makes it actually look the part.

If video.playbackRate is defined, you check the direction parameter passed in—again "-" for back and "+" for forward—and decrease or increase playbackRate accordingly. If the playbackRate is 0, the video is effectively paused and playback stops. Otherwise, you move the video's currentTime backwards or forward by 1.

> **TIP:** Although Safari and Chrome support the playbackRate attribute, they work in different ways. Both support the incrementing of the parameter to fast forward, but Chrome doesn't support rewinding. Safari on the other hand actually starts to play the video backwards, right to the start.

Your simple but slightly more awesome than it was at the start of the chapter media player now has a full set of rather grey but functional buttons and a working progress bar (**Figure 5.7**).

With a bit of jiggery pokery with CSS, you can style the player to your taste and achieve what you see in **Figure 5.8** or perhaps something better.

Just when you thought you were finished with this simple media player, you'll make one final addition to increase its awesomeness—progress bar seek functionality.

> **NOTE:** The code for this styled player and for the unstyled player is available on the website at www.html5multimedia.com.

ADDING A SEEK BAR

Progress bar seek functionality allows users to click anywhere on the progress bar to move the video to that point. No new HTML is needed for this; everything you need to do to add this functionality is all in the JavaScript. You just need to add one event listener and two functions.

Because the interaction will be via a mouse, you need to add an event listener for the mouseup event (which is raised when a user releases the mouse button at the end of a click) to the progress bar:

```
var progressBar = document.getElementById("progressBar");
progressBar.addEventListener("mouseup", function(e)
 →  { setPlayPosition(e.pageX); }, false);
```

This code indicates that the setPlayPosition() function (which takes one parameter—the *x*-coordinate of the mouse position at the time of the click) is called when mouseup is raised.

Define the setPlayPosition() function as:

```
function setPlayPosition(x) {

    var progressBar = document.getElementById("progressBar");

    var value = (x - findPos(progressBar)).toFixed(2);

    var timeToSet = ((video.duration /
     →  progressBar.offsetWidth).toFixed(2) * value).toFixed(2);

    video.currentTime = timeToSet;

}
```

The setPlayPosition() function is where it all happens. You define a handle to the progress bar and then set a variable value based on the *x*-coordinate of the mouse position at the time of the click—minus the real position of the progress bar on the web page (obtained via the findPos() function)—to two decimal places:

findPos() is defined as:

```
function findPos(obj) {
    var curleft = 0;
    if (obj.offsetParent) {
        do { curleft += obj.offsetLeft; } while
    →    (obj = obj.offsetParent);
    }
    return curleft;
}
```

NOTE: The findPos() function finds the real position of an HTML element, taking into account the position of its parents. You can read more about the code behind it at www.quirksmode.org/js/findpos.html.

You calculate the value variable via the findPos() function to get a more accurate reading for the mouse position, because it takes into account the offset position of the progress bar.

Next, you define the timeToSet variable, which will be the actual time value the video will be set to. You calculate this variable by taking the full duration of the video and dividing it by the width of the progress bar. The resulting calculation roughly equates to the pixel position per video unit of time, which you then multiply by value. All the results are obtained to two decimal places.

You then set the video's currentTime variable to this new time value.

Now when a user clicks in the progress bar, the video will move to that position and play will continue/start from there.

The player that you just created is of course HTML5 only, and for browsers that don't support HTML5, such as Internet Explorer 6 to 8, the player won't work. So how can you make it compatible with such browsers? That's what you'll learn next.

NON-HTML5 BROWSERS

To make your player compatible with non-HTML5 browsers, you'll first need to add a Flash resource (as discussed in Chapter 4) to the video element for these browsers to use. Then perform a check to see if the browser supports HTML5 video. If so, you can carry on with all that fancy JavaScript that adds the controls, events, and functions. If the browser doesn't support HTML5 video, you'll hide your custom controls and let the Flash player handle the video playback and provide user controls.

You can check for video browser support by using the following piece of JavaScript:

```
var v = document.createElement("video");
if (v.play) {
    /* ...the browser supports HTML5 video...*/
}
else {
    /*...the browser doesn't support HTML5 video...*/
}
```

This code creates a dummy video element and then checks to see if the play function exists. If not, the browser doesn't support video playback.

WRAPPING UP

You're now familiar with most of the attributes, events, and methods of the HTML5 Media JavaScript API and what they can be used for. You learned how to use them to build a simple HTML5 video player with custom controls that also reacts to changes in the video playback from other sources via events.

Of course, that's not all you can do with the API and your video player, which after all is quite simple and basic. You could take it further and add a playlist that loads videos in the player based on user selection from a list. But that feature is outside the scope of your simple media player.

You styled the final version of your minimal media player (Figure 5.8) via CSS, which was simply a case of adding the styling to the standard HTML elements you used to build up your control set: div, button, and span. The next chapter shows how you can use CSS to style the actual media elements.

6

STYLING **MEDIA** **ELEMENTS** WITH **CSS**

Because the audio and video elements are valid HTML elements, you can treat them the same way as other elements, such as div, header, article, and section. This, of course, means that the audio and video elements can be styled via CSS.

No longer do you need to obtain a Flash player that has the correct or similar colours so that the player fits in with your website's colour scheme (well, except for non-HTML5 browsers of course). Now you can don your CSS hat and use your skills to make these elements look the way you want them to.

As well as the usual CSS declarations that you are familiar with, a number of new ones have surfaced with the advent of CSS3—the latest version of CSS. In this chapter, you'll learn some of the most useful CSS properties and techniques that you can apply to media elements. You'll also learn about browser-vendor prefixed CSS rules and why they're needed.

SIMPLE **CSS STYLING**

FIGURE 6.1 Some simple CSS styling can make the video more aesthetically pleasing.

Cascading Style Sheets (CSS) is a language that is used to describe the presentation of a document written in a markup language, in this case HTML5. CSS basically separates the document content from the document style, which includes colours, background images, fonts, and positioning.

A complete and thorough study of CSS, its syntax, and its properties is outside the scope of this book. If you are new to CSS, check out the many books and online resources available to you to familiarise yourself with the concept.

Before diving into more advanced styling, let's first look at a few simple examples of how you can use basic CSS to style the look of a video element.

To begin, let's take a video, give it a large white border, and centre it in the middle of a web document (**Figure 6.1**).

The code for the video is nothing you haven't seen before:

```
<video controls preload="metadata">
    <source src="parrots-small.mp4" type="video/mp4">
    <source src="parrots-small.webm" type="video/webm">
</video>
```

The basic CSS that's used to achieve the styling is as follows:

```
body {
    background-color:#262626;
    margin:0 auto;
    text-align:center;
}
```

```
video {
    margin-top:100px;
    border:20px solid #fff;
}
```

The body has a background colour of #262626 (a sort of charcoal), and its contents are aligned in the centre. The video element has a thick white border of 20 pixels and is placed 100 pixels from the top of the page. This improves the overall look of the video.

NOTE: You can use `margin:0 auto;` on the video **element if you want to centre videos inside different content** div **columns.**

If you wanted to add a title on top of the video, you could use the usual method of relative positioning and z-indexes to ensure that the title is placed where you want it. The following HTML defines a simple container div, a div containing the title, and then the video element:

```
<div class="container">
    <div class="title">Parrots</div>
    <video controls preload="metadata">
        <source src="parrots-small.mp4" type="video/mp4">
        <source src="parrots-small.webm" type="video/webm">
    </video>
</div>
```

The container div is simply being used to enclose the title div and the video within a certain width:

```
.container {
    width:340px;
}
```

Next, you style the title div, giving it certain dimensions, applying a background colour, centering the text, and transforming the text into uppercase. Let's also give it a position of relative and define the z-index as 2:

```
.title {
    width:200px;
    height:30px;
    background-color:#aaa;
    z-index:2;
    position:relative;
    margin:10px auto;
    border:1px solid #262626;
    text-transform:uppercase;
    text-align:center;
}
```

Then give some dimensions to the video, a position of relative, and a z-index of 1 (less than that of the title div so it will be placed behind it). Apply a negative margin at the top to place it under the title div, and then horizontally centre it inside the container div (via the auto setting):

```
video {
    margin:-35px auto;
    width:305px;
    height:152px;
    border:20px solid #fff;
    position:relative;
    z-index:1;
}
```

FIGURE 6.2 A title div is placed on top of the video element.

FIGURE 6.3 The video with a white background.

The result is shown in **Figure 6.2**.

If you need to define a video element that is bigger than the video it contains (e.g., videos of different sizes might be loaded into the element), the video might letterbox. You can apply a background colour to the video element, which will then fill the empty space:

```
video {
    margin:20px;
    background-color:#fff;
    width:305px;
    height:200px;
}
```

Here the background colour is defined as #fff (white), and the result is shown in **Figure 6.3**.

The preceding examples were nothing spectacular and relatively easy. However, they show that you can manipulate and style the video element the same way as any other HTML element using the CSS knowledge that you already have.

Next up are a few CSS3-specific examples.

ADVANCED **WHIZZYNESS**
WITH **CSS3**

CSS3, the latest version of CSS to emerge, has a whole host of new rules and properties that its predecessor, CSS2.1, didn't have. And you can use these new features to style HTML elements to your heart's content.

A study and list of these rules and properties are outside the scope of this book, but you can view the specification at www.w3.org/TR/CSS.

Some of the more interesting properties that add new functionality are discussed in the following sections, and as usual, contain complete examples.

TIP: Two fantastic resources for CSS3 and examples of how you can use its various bits and pieces are CSS3.info at http://www.css3.info and Dev.Opera at http://dev.opera.com/articles/css.

OPACITY

You can, should you want to, make your video transparent using the CSS3 `opacity` property. This property takes a value between 0 and 1; 0 is invisible and 1 is opaque:

```
video {
    opacity:0.5;
}
```

This piece of CSS makes the video 50-percent transparent (**Figure 6.4**).

You could then bring the video to 100-percent opacity on hover by using the following:

```
video:hover {
    opacity:1;
}
```

Opacity works in the latest versions of Firefox, Opera, Internet Explorer, and Safari. Chrome renders the video controls transparent but not the video.

FIGURE 6.4 This video is 50-percent transparent in Firefox 5.

GRADIENT

Another new addition to CSS3 is the ability to define a gradient (blending from one colour to another) as the background image of an element. Specifying gradients makes use of another CSS3 property, rgba colour definitions.

Previously in CSS, colours could be defined through common names (e.g., white), colour hex codes (e.g., #ffffff), or rgb colour definitions where you define the individual red, green, and blue values of the colour, (e.g., rgb(255,255,255)). These colour definitions are of course still completely valid in CSS3, but you can also use a new rule, rgba. Similar to rgb, rgba also allows you to define the alpha channel—that is, the opacity value for the colour in addition to the red, green, and blue values. For example, a definition of rgba(255,255,255,0.5) defines a white colour with 50-percent opacity. Gradients make use of this as you will see next.

You can also use a gradient with a video, but you can't apply it to the actual element because, as a background image, the video would always and correctly be on top and therefore hide most or all of the background. You can, however, add the gradient to a div that you then place on top of the video element like this:

```
<video controls preload="metadata">
    <source src="parrots-small.mp4" type="video/mp4">
    <source src="parrots-small.webm" type="video/webm">
</video>
<div class="gradient"></div>
```

Then give the video a relative position and a z-index of 1. Give the gradient div a relative position, the same dimensions as the video, and a z-index of 2 (so it remains on top of the video element), and apply the gradient:

```
.gradient {
    width:305px;
    height:152px;
    margin:-187px 30px 30px;
    position:relative;
    z-index:2;
    background-image: -webkit-linear-gradient(
        top,
        rgba(255,255,255,0),
        rgba(255,255,255,1)
    );
    background-image: -moz-linear-gradient(
        top,
        rgba(255,255,255,0),
        rgba(255,255,255,1)
    );
    background-image: -o-linear-gradient(
        top,
        rgba(255,255,255,0),
        rgba(255,255,255,1)
    );
    background-image: linear-gradient(
        top,
        rgba(255,255,255,0),
        rgba(255,255,255,1)
    );
}
```

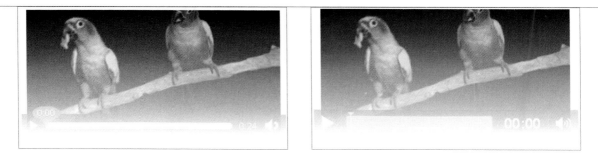

FIGURE 6.5 The video with the gradient applied in Firefox 5 (left) and Chrome 13 (right).

The gradient colours are defined using the new CSS3 rgba colour-setting rule mentioned earlier. The colour definitions used in the preceding example have the "from" colour defined with an opacity of 0 (transparent), and the "to" colour is defined with an opacity of 1 (opaque).

Notice that there are four different definitions for the gradient: one with the -moz prefix (Mozilla Firefox specific), one with -webkit (WebKit browser specific; Safari and Chrome), one with -o (Opera), and one without any browser-specific prefix, which is the CSS3 definition but might not yet be supported.

> **TIP:** It's always a good idea to provide browser-specific CSS definitions (if they exist) as well as the actual specification version to ensure that all browsers that are capable of using the style rule will.

The definitions generally take the format:

```
position, gradient-from-colour, gradient-to-colour
```

You can see how the gradient looks in **Figure 6.5**. Notice that the controls are covered and cannot be used, so you should implement them via the JavaScript API, as described in Chapter 5.

Gradient works in Firefox, Chrome, and Safari.

> **NOTE:** You can do more with CSS3 linear gradient rules than is shown in the examples, but any further explanation is outside the scope of the book. You can read more about CSS3 linear gradients at http://dev.opera.com/articles/view/css3-linear-gradients.

FIGURE 6.6 A video element with lovely rounded corners.

ROUNDED CORNERS

Rounded corners were once the bane of the web developer's life, with many an hour spent fiddling with background images to add rounded corners to an HTML element. That pain is relieved in CSS3 with the addition of border-radius, which allows you to add rounded corners to any HTML element, and that includes the multimedia elements:

```
video {
    -moz-border-radius:20px;
    -webkit-border-radius:20px;
    border-radius:20px;
}
```

Once again, there are a number of browser-specific definitions, but each gives the element a rounded-corner radius of 20 pixels (**Figure 6.6**).

At the moment, rounded corners on media elements currently only work in Firefox.

SHADOW

In conjunction with rounded corners, adding a shadow to an HTML element is another common web developer task. And once again. CSS3 comes to the rescue and adds it to the specification.

Using the following code, you can add a shadow colour of #999 to the 10 pixels at the bottom and right of the video with a spread of 5 pixels:

FIGURE 6.7 A video with a drop shadow in Chrome 13.

```
video {
    -moz-box-shadow: 10px 10px 5px #999;
    -webkit-box-shadow: 10px 10px 5px #999;
    box-shadow: 10px 10px 5px #999;
}
```

The result is shown in **Figure 6.7**.

ROUNDED **CORNERS** PLUS **SHADOW**

Combining rounded corners with shadow and applying them to a video element has an odd effect in all browsers other than Firefox.

Firefox renders the properties correctly, but other browsers ignore the rounded corners on the video element and instead show the rounded corners on the shadow (**Figure 6.8**)!

FIGURE 6.8 The video with rounded corners and a drop shadow rendered in Firefox (left) and then in Chrome (right).

Not only can you apply a drop shadow and rounded corners to the video element, but you can also apply them to the audio element:

```
<audio controls>
    <source src="sayHello.ogg" type="audio/ogg">
    <source src="sayHello.mp4" type="audio/mp4">
</audio>
```

This audio element is then styled like this:

```
audio {
    border-radius:10px;
    box-shadow:10px 10px 5px #888;
}
```

The preceding audio element example displays best in Firefox (**Figure 6.9**); other browsers don't apply the rounded corners to the audio element.

SIZING YOUR CONTENT

Two new properties in the CSS3 specification allow you to specify how replaced content within replaced elements, such as images and video, are contained. You might want your video content to occupy a space of certain dimensions but want the aspect ratio to be maintained rather than stretching or squashing the content. Equally, you may actually want the video content to be squashed or stretched! The two properties that allow you to define how you want the video content to be rendered are the object-fit and object-position properties.

OBJECT-FIT

object-fit specifies how the element should be scaled relative to the container, using its height and width. object-fit can have a number of values:

- fill   The contents fill the container.

- contain   The contents fill the container, and the aspect ratio of the multimedia element is maintained.

- cover   The contents fill the container completely.

- none   The contents fill the entire container irrespective of the aspect ratio, so some stretching may occur.

- scale-down   Apply whichever one of none or contain would result in a smaller size.

It's quite difficult to understand what each object-fit value means without actually seeing its result. So let's look at an example of all of them using five videos:

```
<video id="v1" width="200" height="200" preload="metadata">
    <source src="parrots-tiny.mp4" type="video/mp4">
    <source src="parrots-small.webm" type="video/webm">
</video>
<video id="v2" width="200" height="200" preload="metadata">
    <source src="parrots-small.mp4" type="video/mp4">
    <source src="parrots-small.webm" type="video/webm">
</video>
<video id="v3" width="200" height="200" preload="metadata">
    <source src="parrots-small.mp4" type="video/mp4">
    <source src="parrots-small.webm" type="video/webm">
</video>
<video id="v4" width="200" height="200" preload="metadata">
    <source src="parrots-small.mp4" type="video/mp4">
```

```
        <source src="parrots-small.webm" type="video/webm">
</video>
<video id="v5" width="200" height="200" preload="metadata">
    <source src="parrots-small.mp4" type="video/mp4">
    <source src="parrots-small.webm" type="video/webm">
</video>
```

Style the videos like this:

```
video {
    border:1px solid #000;
    display:block;
    margin-bottom:10px;
}
video#v1 {
    -o-object-fit:none;
}
video#v2 {
    -o-object-fit:contain;
}
video#v3 {
    -o-object-fit:cover;
}
video#v4 {
    -o-object-fit:fill;
}
video#v5 {
    -o-object-fit:scale-down;
}
```

FIGURE 6.10 The video element uses the object-fit:fill setting to enclose the content.

FIGURE 6.11 The video element uses the object-fit:contain setting to enclose the content.

FIGURE 6.12 The video element uses the object-fit:cover setting to enclose the content.

FIGURE 6.13 The video element uses the object-fit:none setting to enclose the content.

FIGURE 6.14 The video element uses the object-fit:scale-down setting to enclose the content.

Figures 6.10 through 6.14 show how the preceding code displays the videos in Opera 11.50.

Incidentally, this method of positioning objects currently works only in Opera and needs to use the Opera-specific property o-object-fit.

OBJECT-POSITION

object-position indicates the alignment of the element within the container. This CSS rule takes the same values as the well-known background-position property and is used in the same way to define where the element should be placed.

Using four of the previous video definitions, you could position them as follows:

```
<video id="v1" preload="metadata">
    <source src="parrots-tiny.mp4" type="video/mp4">
    <source src="parrots-tiny.webm" type="video/webm">
</video>
<video id="v2" preload="metadata">
    <source src="parrots-tiny.mp4" type="video/mp4">
    <source src="parrots-tiny.webm" type="video/webm">
</video>
<video id="v3" preload="metadata">
    <source src="parrots-tiny.mp4" type="video/mp4">
    <source src="parrots-tiny.webm" type="video/webm">
</video>
<video id="v4" preload="metadata">
    <source src="parrots-tiny.mp4" type="video/mp4">
    <source src="parrots-tiny.webm" type="video/webm">
</video>
```

Style the videos as follows but with a different -o-object-position CSS rule defined for each video:

```
video {
    border:1px solid #000;
    display:block;
    margin-bottom:10px;
    width:300px;
    height:180px;
    -o-object-fit:none;
}
video#v1 {
    -o-object-position:top left;
}
video#v2 {
    -o-object-position:right center;
}
video#v3 {
    -o-object-position:right bottom;
}
video#v4 {
    -o-object-position:center;
}
```

You've now defined four videos, each with a border and specified dimensions but with different settings for object-position.

> **NOTE:** The object-position property is currently only supported in Opera, which requires the browser-specific -o-object-position property.

FIGURE 6.15 The video's content is placed using `object-position:top left`.

FIGURE 6.16 The video's content is placed using `object-position:right center`.

FIGURE 6.17 The video's content is placed using `object-position:right bottom`.

FIGURE 6.18 The video's content is placed using `object-position:center`.

Figures 6.15 through **6.18** show how each of the videos render in Opera 11.50. You can apply and use several CSS3 rules with the video element. Those discussed in this section just give you a taste of what is available to you. You're encouraged to explore others on your own.

Some WebKit-specific settings are not part of the CSS3 specification, but they do exist and do some cool stuff. We'll look at some of those next.

TIP: You can read more about the `object-fit` and `object-position` CSS3 properties at http://dev.w3.org/csswg/css3-images/#object-fit and http://dev.w3.org/csswg/css3-images/#object-position.

FIGURE 6.19 A video on auto-play reflected beneath itself in Chrome 13.

Two fun WebKit-specific properties are well worth looking at: `reflect` and `mask`. It is hoped that they will become part of a wider specification. Even if they don't, you can wow your WebKit browser users now with the effects they produce.

REFLECT

The `-webkit-box-reflect` property allows you to specify a reflection on an HTML element. Here, you'll apply it to a video:

```
video {
    -webkit-box-reflect:below 0px;
}
```

The short code snippet defines a reflection immediately below the video in question (**Figure 6.19**). The controls in the video have been removed because they will also be included in the reflection, which is not ideal; instead, you should implement them via the Media JavaScript API.

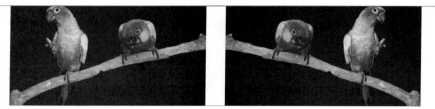

FIGURE 6.20 The video is reflected on the right side, 30 pixels away, in Chrome 13.

You could also reflect the video 30 pixels to the right (**Figure 6.20**).

```
video {
    -webkit-box-reflect:right 30px;
}
```

MASK

You can also add a mask over the video using the -webkit-mask-box-image property. To do this, you need to create a mask image, which should be the same dimensions as the video. The mask should also be transparent where you want to hide the video and opaque where you want the video to show through.

NOTE: Chrome 13 requires the image mask to be opaque where you want to hide the video and transparent where you want the video to show through. This was also a requirement in Safari 5.0.5 but was recently changed in version 5.1.

Then you simply assign the URL of that image to the -webkit-mask-box-image property within the video element CSS rule set and supply a background colour that will fill the opaque areas of the mask image:

```
video {
    -webkit-mask-box-image:url('oval-mask.png');
    background-color:#262626;
}
```

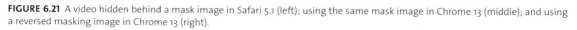

FIGURE 6.21 A video hidden behind a mask image in Safari 5.1 (left); using the same mask image in Chrome 13 (middle); and using a reversed masking image in Chrome 13 (right).

This example uses a simple mask image in the shape of an oval; the oval area is where the video should appear (**Figure 6.21**).

If the controls are hidden or partially hidden behind the mask image, they will be inaccessible; therefore, you should remove the default control set and implement it via JavaScript.

If you wanted users to view a video through a particular image for extra effect—for example, to view a video of the sea through a porthole—you could use a mask image.

It's a shame that the `reflect` and `mask` properties are WebKit specific. But who knows; perhaps some day they'll be standardised and will make it into the next CSS specification.

> **TIP:** You can read more about using the `reflect` and `mask` properties at http://designshack.co.uk/articles/css/mastering-css-reflections-in-webkit.

WRAPPING **UP**

You learned how you can create HTML5 multimedia elements just like any other HTML elements within your web document and style and position them in the same way, too. This chapter has only given you a taste of what you can do when styling your elements. Be sure to experiment with styling and see what you can discover and what results you can achieve.

You also learned about some of the new functionality that comes with a few of the latest CSS3 properties. But CSS3 extends a bit further. Chapter 7 discusses transitions, transforms, and animation in CSS3.

7

TRANSITIONS, TRANSFORMS, AND ANIMATION

You know you can use CSS to style your multimedia elements, but CSS3 provides some new and exciting additions. Using three of these new additions—transitions, transforms, and animation—you can create visual enhancements via CSS without the need for any fancy JavaScript. Because such features are considered presentational, it's ideal that they're part of CSS.

This chapter briefly introduces you to some of the aspects of CSS3 transitions, transforms, and animation. You'll learn how to use and combine them to add dynamic effects to your layout.

USING **TRANSITIONS**

One of the dictionary definitions for a transition is a "passage from one form, state, style, or place to another." This is the same with HTML elements and particularly with styling. It is either this colour or that colour, placed at this position or that position. There is no in-between state; it is one or the other. Transitions add an in-between state between one style, position, or state and another.

For example, let's say you have an HTML element that you have defined set dimensions for and that on hover you want that particular element to increase in size. This is relatively simple to do with the following CSS applied to an HTML img element:

```
img{
    width:183px;
    height:164px;
}
img:hover {
    width:275px;
    height:246px;
}
```

And here is the image that the preceding CSS is applied to:

```
<img src="football-small.jpg" alt="Colour football" />
```

NOTE: All the coding examples used in this chapter are online at www.html5multimedia.com.

Hovering over this image will result in it jumping from 183 × 164 pixels in size to 275 × 246 pixels and back again (when you move the mouse away). The transition between the two states is nonexistent, because the image switches from one size to the other instantaneously (**Figure 7.1**).

This is where CSS Transitions come in. The W3C describes transitions this way:

"CSS Transitions allows property changes in CSS values to occur smoothly over a specified duration."

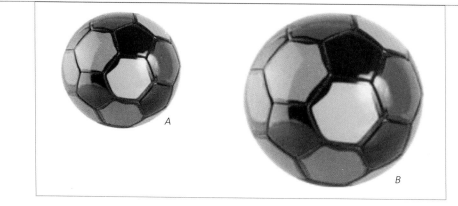

FIGURE 7.1 The ball jumps in size from one state (A) to another (B) on hover.

Using the previous example, you can add a transition rule to the img element so that it gradually increases in size to 275 × 246 pixels rather than jumping from its original size to the new larger size.

TIP: CSS Transitions are supported by all the major browsers, although you should use browser-specific CSS rules to ensure compatibility.

To create this transition, you'll use some of the transition properties listed in **Table 7.1**.

TABLE 7.1 CSS3 Transition Properties

NAME	DESCRIPTION
transition-property	Specifies the name(s) of the transition to which the transition is to be applied (e.g., background, color, font-size, none, or all).
transition-duration	Defines the length of time in seconds that the transition will actually take. A value of 0s indicates that the transition is to take place immediately.
transition-timing-function	Specifies the function to be used in calculating the intermediate values during the transition. There are a number of predefined values for this property: ease, linear, ease-in, ease-out, ease-in-out, and cubic-bezier(), which allows you to define your own.
transition-delay	Defines when the transition will start. A value of 0s, the default setting, causes the transition to begin immediately.

Given that you should add all the different vendor-specific rules for each transition property specified, this can lead to rather a long list! For Mozilla alone, defining a transition rule could take three lines:

```
-moz-transition-property:all;
-moz-transition-duration:1s;
-moz-transition-timing-function:ease;
```

TIP: For a list of all the properties that you can apply transitions to, see www.w3.org/TR/css3-transitions/#properties-from-css, and for more on the transition timing functions, see www.w3.org/TR/css3-transitions/#transition-timing-function.

Adding rules for the other three vendors plus the nonvendor-specific rule definition would make that 15 lines of CSS just for one transition! Fortunately, you can get around this by using the shorthand rule, which allows you to define the various properties together, for example:

```
-moz-transition: all 1s ease;
```

So, using the previous transition rule information and providing all the different vendor-specific shorthand rules, you can define the transition like this:

```
img {
    width:183px;
    height:164px;
    -webkit-transition: all 1s ease;
    -moz-transition: all 1s ease;
    -o-transition: all 1s ease;
    -ms-transition: all 1s ease;
    transition: all 1s ease;
}
```

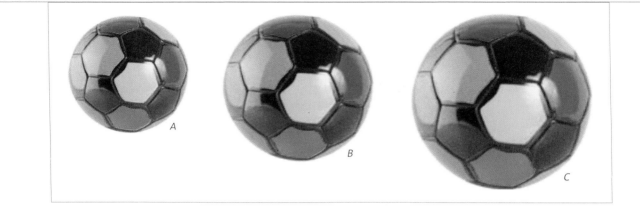

You put the `transition` rule on the normal state of the element in question rather than the `:hover` state. The reason is that you might want the transition to apply to all states on this element, such as `:focus`.

Now the transition between the two states on hover is much smoother as the image gradually changes from one size to the next (**Figure 7.2**).

FIGURE 7.2 Although you'll have to use your imagination here, the image now smoothly increases from one size (A) to the other (C) with transition states in between (represented by B).

USING TRANSITIONS WITH AUDIO AND VIDEO

Because you can apply transitions to any HTML element, you can of course use `transition` with the audio and video elements:

```
video {
    width:146px;
    height:76px;
    -webkit-transition: all 1s ease;
    -moz-transition: all 1s ease;
    -o-transition: all 1s ease;
    -ms-transition: all 1s ease;
    transition: all 1s ease;
}
```

A

B

C

FIGURE 7.3 On hover, the video smoothly transitions from one size (A) to another (C) with transitions in between (represented by B).

```
video:hover {
    width:292px;
    height:152px;
}
```

Try to visualise how the video smoothly increases in size from 146 × 76 to 292 × 152 (**Figure 7.3**).

STYLING WITH CSS TRANSITIONS

With CSS Transitions, you can style your video in different ways to create a better experience for your users. For example, suppose you have a video that you've styled with a drop shadow, like this:

```
<video controls preload="metadata">
    <source src="parrots-small.mp4" type="video/mp4">
    <source src="parrots-small.webm" type="video/webm">
</video>
video {
    margin:100px;
    -moz-box-shadow: 5px 5px 5px #999;
    -webkit-box-shadow: 5px 5px 5px #999;
    box-shadow: 5px 5px 5px #999;
}
```

FIGURE 7.4 When the user hovers on the video (left), the drop shadow increases smoothly (right).

But you want to increase the drop shadow when a user hovers over the video. Nothing fancy; you just want to add a subtle responsive action back to the user. You'd define the hover state for the video, and then add the transition to the normal state of the video element:

```
video {
    margin:100px;
    -moz-box-shadow: 5px 5px 5px #999;
    -webkit-box-shadow: 5px 5px 5px #999;
    box-shadow: 5px 5px 5px #999;
    -webkit-transition: all 1s ease;
    -moz-transition: all 1s ease;
    -o-transition: all 1s ease;
    -ms-transition: all 1s ease;
    transition: all 1s ease;
}
video:hover {
    -moz-box-shadow: 10px 10px 5px #999;
    -webkit-box-shadow: 10px 10px 5px #999;
    box-shadow: 10px 10px 5px #999;
}
```

Now the shadow increases ever so slightly on the hover state, creating subtle but effective feedback to the user (**Figure 7.4**).

FADING TRANSITIONS

You can also use a transition to fade the video from an opacity value of 0.5 to 1 on :hover and :focus. You might want to do this if you have a list of videos displayed on the screen at the same time and want the video that the user hovers over and plays to become opaque:

```
video {
    opacity:0.5;
    -webkit-transition: opacity 2s linear;
    -moz-transition: opacity 2s linear;
    -o-transition: opacity 2s linear;
    -ms-transition: opacity 2s linear;
    transition: opacity 2s linear;
}
video:hover, video:focus {
    opacity:1;
}
```

This time the duration is increased to 2 seconds, and the transition targets the opacity value only (rather than all, as the previous examples did) (**Figure 7.5**).

NOTE: Chrome seems to have issues with transitioning opacity on the video element; it fades only the controls rather than the entire element.

A

B

C

FIGURE 7.5 The video starts with an opacity of 50 percent (A) to fully visible (C) on hover, with a transition in between (represented by B).

The previous examples give you an idea of what you can do with CSS Transitions—create new states for the element and transition to them smoothly.

But that's not all you can do. You can also apply two-dimensional and three-dimensional transformations to HTML elements.

TIP: You can read more about CSS3 Transitions in the specification at www.w3.org/TR/css3-transitions.

EXPLORING **2D TRANSFORMS**

FIGURE 7.6 The video scales by a factor of 1.5 on hover, moving from a small size (left) to a larger size (right).

A transform is defined as changing the appearance or form of something. The "something" in this case, of course, is an HTML element. An HTML element is positioned somewhere in a web document, and its position is usually determined by properties and values in CSS. But you might want to transform the HTML element in some way, either its position or appearance, and CSS Transforms allow you to do this.

There are two types of CSS Transforms, 2D and 3D. Let's first take a look at 2D Transforms.

2D Transforms allow elements to be transformed in two-dimensional space. With CSS 2D Transforms, you can scale, rotate, skew, and translate an HTML element within the space it's defined—that is, the web document.

SCALING A VIDEO

The best way to start looking at 2D Transforms is to work through a simple example. Using the colourful parrots video, you'll add a scaling transform to scale the video's size on the hover state of the video:

```
<video controls preload="metadata">
    <source src="parrots-tiny.mp4" type="video/mp4">
    <source src="parrots-tiny.webm" type="video/webm">
</video>
```

To add the transform, you use the transform rule, but again, vendor-specific rules are required to ensure the best browser coverage.

You first need to specify which transform you want to use. In this case, you'll use the scale transform, which takes one parameter that indicates the scale by

NOTE: Like CSS3 Transitions, 2D Transforms are well supported across modern browsers, as long as you use vendor-specific CSS rules.

A

B

C

which you want the element to be transformed. A value greater than 1 scales up; any value less than 1 scales down. The values work like percentages; scale(0.75) indicates a scale of 75 percent, whereas scale(1.25) would indicate a scale of 125 percent. In this example, you'll scale up the video by a value of 1.5 (150 percent):

FIGURE 7.7 The scale transform is now much smoother and nicer to look at as it moves from a small size (A) to a larger size (C) via an in-between state (B).

```
video:hover {

    -webkit-transform:scale(1.5);

    -moz-transform:scale(1.5);

    -o-transform:scale(1.5);

    -ms-transform:scale(1.5);

    -transform:scale(1.5);

}
```

Now when the user hovers over the video, it will scale upward by a factor of 1.5 (**Figure 7.6**).

But like the first transition example earlier in the chapter, the transition between the states is clunky and ugly. So, what can you do? Well, add a transition of course!

Using what you've already learned, you can apply a simple transition to the normal state of the video element to make the scale transform action much smoother (**Figure 7.7**):

```
video {

    -webkit-transition: all 1s ease;

    -moz-transition: all 1s ease;

    -o-transition: all 1s ease;

    -ms-transition: all 1s ease;

    -transition: all 1s ease;

}
```

FIGURE 7.8 The video is rotated 5 degrees in an anticlockwise direction.

Of course, scale isn't the only transformation available; you can also rotate the element, which is what you'll do next.

ROTATING A VIDEO

This time you'll rotate the video's normal state, so no transition or hover state rules are required.

Using the same transform rule as you did earlier, you simply indicate that you want the element to be rotated rather than scaled. For example, you might have a number of videos on a page and you want them to look as though they're scattered randomly on the page, each at a slightly different angle.

The rotate transform also takes one parameter: the number of degrees in which the element is to be rotated. A positive value rotates it clockwise; a negative value rotates it anticlockwise:

```
video {
    -webkit-transform:rotate(-5deg);
    -moz-transform:rotate(-5deg);
    -o-transform:rotate(-5deg);
    -ms-transform:rotate(-5deg);
    -transform:rotate(-5deg);
}
```

Here, the video is rotated 5 degrees anticlockwise (**Figure 7.8**).

And the goodness doesn't end there! You can also skew the video should this be what you want to achieve.

FIGURE 7.9 A video with a drop shadow skewed 15 degrees to the left.

SKEWING A VIDEO

Using the video with an added drop shadow, you can skew it 15 degrees to the left:

```
video {
    -webkit-transform:skew(15deg);
    -moz-transform:skew(15deg);
    -o-transform:skew(15deg);
    -ms-transform:skew(15deg);
    -transform:skew(15deg);
    -moz-box-shadow: -10px 10px 5px #999;
    -webkit-box-shadow: -10px 10px 5px #999;
    box-shadow: -10px 10px 5px #999;
}
```

A negative skew value would skew the video to the right. **Figure 7.9** shows the result of skewing to the left.

The skew transform can also take two parameters, allowing you to specify two different skew values for the X and Y axes.

Oh, and there's more! You can also translate an element from one position to another.

TRANSLATING A VIDEO

The translate transform takes two parameters, relativeX and relativeY. These two parameters will move the element to the required position specified relative to its normal position without affecting the elements around it.

In this example, let's use two videos beside each other in a div with a black border. On its hover state, each video will move 50 pixels to the right and down from its current position:

```
<div class="container">
    <video controls preload="metadata">
        <source src="parrots-tiny.mp4" type="video/mp4">
        <source src="parrots-tiny.webm" type="video/webm">
    </video>
    <video controls>
        <source src="parrots-tiny.mp4" type="video/mp4">
        <source src="parrots-tiny.webm" type="video/webm">
    </video>
</div>
video:hover {
    -webkit-transform:translate(50px,50px);
    -moz-transform:translate(50px,50px);
    -o-transform:translate(50px,50px);
    -ms-transform:translate(50px,50px);
    transform:translate(50px,50px);
}
```

If you wanted to translate the videos to different positions, you could do so by giving each video a unique identifier and then specifying different translate values for each video via this identifier.

Combining what you learned earlier, you can also add a border, a drop shadow, and an easing transition to the videos to give them a smooth transform:

```
video {
    margin-right:10px;
    border:1px solid #000;
    -moz-box-shadow: -10px 10px 5px #999;
```

FIGURE 7.10 The videos sit beside each other in their normal state.

FIGURE 7.11 The first video's hover state is triggered, and the video makes its way to its new translated position.

FIGURE 7.12 The first video settles into its new temporary position. Note how it hasn't affected the position of the second video.

```
    -webkit-box-shadow: -10px 10px 5px #999;

    box-shadow: -10px 10px 5px #999;

    -webkit-transition: all 1s ease;

    -moz-transition: all 1s ease;

    -o-transition: all 1s ease;

    -ms-transition: all 1s ease;

    -transition: all 1s ease;

}
```

Figures 7.10 through 7.12 give you an idea of how the transform would work.

TIP: Most of the CSS3 2D Transform functions also have X and Y equivalents, such as scaleX() and skewY(), which allow you to work on one axis only. The matrix() function also exists, but it is quite complex! You can read more about these and 2D Transforms in general at www.w3.org/TR/css3-2d-transforms.

CSS 2D Transforms can be quite useful to achieve some nifty effects. But recall that there are two types of CSS Transforms. Let's now have a look at 3D Transforms.

PLAYING WITH 3D TRANSFORMS

3D Transforms are, of course, quite similar to 2D Transforms except they deal with three dimensions rather than two. Unfortunately, 3D Transforms are poorly supported across browsers; only WebKit browsers currently provide any support at all. It is for this reason that they are only briefly mentioned here.

The W3C specification mentions that although a 3D Transform:

"...uses a three-dimensional coordinate system, the elements themselves are not three-dimensional objects. Instead, they exist on a two-dimensional plane (a flat surface) and have no depth."

You can give elements a perspective via the perspective property, which sets the perspective (in pixels) from which an element is viewed. This gives a sense of depth, which causes elements farther away from the viewer to appear smaller.

TIP: Applying perspective to an element does not apply to the element itself, only its children.

You can also rotate elements around the three different axes of a 3D plane using the rotate3D(x, y, z, rotation-degree) function. For example, to apply a 25-degree rotation around the Y axis, you'd use rotate3d(0, 1, 0, 25deg). Each of the x, y, and z parameters takes a 1 or 0, which indicates whether to rotate around that axis or not.

Using the scattered videos on a page example mentioned earlier, you might want to add some depth for WebKit users. Let's look at a simple example that shows the two properties just mentioned to give you an idea of how they work.

NOTES: You can read more about 3D Transforms in the W3C specification at www.w3.org/TR/css3-3d-transforms.

Because WebKit browsers are currently the only ones that support 3D Transforms, only the WebKit-specific CSS3 properties are used in the example in this section.

To begin, define a div with a "main" class, which also contains another div with a "bg" class that contains the video:

```
<div class="main">
    <div class="bg">
```

```
        <video controls preload="metadata">
            <source src="parrots-small.mp4" type="video/mp4">
            <source src="parrots-small.webm" type="video/webm">
        </video>
    </div>
</div>
```

Then define positioning for each of these elements in the CSS and also give the video a drop shadow:

```
div.main {
    position:absolute;
    top:50%;
    left:50%;
    margin-left:-350px;
    margin-top:-233px;
}
div.bg {
    height:246px;
    width:380px;
    background-color:#aaa;
}
video {
    width:292px;
    position:absolute;
    top:50px;
    left:50px;
    -webkit-box-shadow:-10px 10px 5px #888;
}
```

FIGURE 7.13 The appearance of the elements in Safari 5.1.

There is no sign of the 3D Transform at the moment, because it hasn't been applied yet (**Figure 7.13**)!

The reason behind the outer div is that you want to apply perspective to it, so that it affects the elements within, in this case the bg div and the video. So, let's apply a perspective of 1000:

```
div.main {
    position:absolute;
    top:50%;
    left:50%;
    margin-left:-350px;
    margin-top:-233px;
    -webkit-perspective:1000;
}
```

This perspective doesn't have any visual effect on the elements, but it will when you add the next and final CSS rule. Add a rotation transform around the Y axis with a 40-degree angle to the div with the bg class:

```
div.bg {
    height:246px;
    width:380px;
    background-color:#aaa;
    -webkit-transform:rotate3d(0, 1, 0, 40deg);
}
```

FIGURE 7.14 The video and background div are rotated at a 40-degree angle around the Y axis in Safari 5.1.

FIGURE 7.15 The same elements and degree of rotation are shown around the X and Y axes.

Figure 7.14 shows how the elements are rendered around the Y axis, and **Figure 7.15** shows the same video rotating around both axes.

The preceding example shows only a small slice of what you can do with 3D Transforms, but it should give you a general gist of what you can achieve.

Because of the limited browser support, I'd recommend not using 3D Transforms at the moment. However, they're definitely worth playing about with to see what you can do with them, as long as you use a WebKit browser. When browser support increases, you'll no doubt see a lot more about 3D Transforms!

> **TIP:** For more information about transforms and 3D Transforms, see the Safari Developer Library at http://developer.apple.com/library/safari/#documentation/InternetWeb/Conceptual/SafariVisualEffectsProgGuide/Transforms/Transforms.html.

With transitions and transforms under your belt, it's time to explore another piece of the CSS3 family, animations.

The CSS3 specification introduces the idea of defined animations, which allow you to specify the values that CSS properties of particular HTML elements will take over a given time interval. This sequence of values, when strung together over the specified time interval, causes the HTML element in question to become animated.

The W3C specification puts it this way:

"CSS Animations allow an author to modify CSS property values over time."

"Values over time" implies that you need to define certain values for different time periods, which you do via the key to CSS Animations, *Keyframes*.

@KEYFRAMES

Keyframes allow you to define functions within the CSS in which you can specify CSS rules for start, end, and intermediary states for an HTML element. To specify such a rule, you use the @keyframes keyword followed by a unique identifier or function name. This is then followed by a set of CSS rules contained within curly braces that specify the different frames of the animation, that is, how the animated element will be moved, rotated, scaled, and so on at different points in the animation.

For example, a very simple Keyframes animation function that moves an element from side to side could be defined as follows:

```
@keyframes shake {
    0% {
        left:5px;
    }
    25% {
        left:10px;
    }
    50% {
        left:15px;
    }
```

```
    75% {
        left:20px;
    }
    100% {
        left:25px
    }
}
```

In the Keyframes function shake, five different time frames are defined; each one contains a different left CSS definition. So at each time frame, the element should have animated to that new position.

You could also write this using the from and to properties, which allow you to specify the start and end states of the animation:

```
@keyframes shake {
    from {
        left:5px;
    }
    to {
        left:25px;
    }
}
```

The preceding definition has the same effect as the earlier definition but is obviously shorter. This can be useful if the animation is a simple one; you can let the browser work out the in-between states.

To actually define an animation, you use a combination of the properties listed in **Table 7.2** on the next page.

TABLE 7.2 CSS3 Animation Properties

PROPERTY	DESCRIPTION
animation-name	Identifies the animation name(s) to apply. Each name should be a defined Keyframe animation function.
animation-duration	Defines the length of time it should take for the animation to complete one cycle.
animation-timing-function	Defines how the animation will progress over one cycle of its durations. It can be one of a number of predefined values: ease, linear, ease-in, ease-out, ease-in-out, or cubic-bezier(). Note that these are the same values that can be used for a transition-timing-function as mentioned in Table 7.1.
animation-iteration-count	Specifies the number of iterations the animation is to perform. Can be set to infinite, which will cause the animation to loop continuously.
animation-direction	Defines whether or not the animation should play in reverse on alternate cycles. Valid values are normal and alternate. A value of normal is the default.
animation-delay	Indicates when the animation will start. Allows a delay to be added to the beginning of the animation if required. A value of 0s, the default, causes the animation to begin immediately.
animation-fill-mode	Indicates what values are applied by the animation outside of the time it is executing. By default, the values contained within the animation frames are not persisted once the animation is complete. Setting this value can override that by using one of four different values: • none. None of the values persist outside of the animation. This is the default. • backwards. Values defined in the first frame will be persisted once the animation is complete. • forwards. Values defined in the final frame will be persisted once the animation is complete. • both. Values in both the first and final frame will be persisted when the animation is complete.

NOTE: The animation-play-state, which defines whether an animation is running or paused, is also currently defined in the CSS3 Animations specification but most likely will be removed in the near future (www.w3.org/TR/css3-animations/#the-animation-play-state-property).

As with transitions, creating the vendor-specific definitions could lead to quite a long set of rules, so once again using the shorthand notation, in this case animation, is the best course of action:

```
-webkit-animation:shake 5s 1 ease;
```

This CSS snippet defines the shake Keyframes animation to be used, with a duration of 5 seconds for one iteration, and uses the ease animation timing function.

NOTE: Support for CSS Animations is currently limited to WebKit browsers and Firefox 4+. Therefore, once again, vendor-specific CSS rules are required to make CSS Animations work.

Moving on from this simple moving animation, let's take a look at how you might use a rotation within an animation sequence.

ANIMATED VIDEO COVER

Using a combination of CSS Transforms and Animations, let's put together a simple example that starts with a covered video, and on click, the cover spins away revealing the video underneath.

You first need to define the HTML markup:

```
<div class="container">
    <div id="cover" class="cover"></div>
    <div class="bg">
        <video poster="sintel-poster.jpg" preload="metadata" controls>
            <source src="sintel-small.mp4" type="video/mp4">
            <source src="sintel-small.webm" type="video/webm">
        </video>
    </div>
</div>
```

The container div contains the cover div, which you'll be animating, and a bg div, which contains the definition for the video. Note that the video in question has a poster image defined, uses the browser's default controls, and also hints that the browser is to only preload the video's metadata.

NOTE: The video used in the video cover animation example is *Sintel* by the Blender Foundation and the Durian Open Movie Project. You can read more about it at www.sintel.org.

Next, you need to define the CSS and concentrate on the way the HTML elements actually look; you'll add the animations and transforms later.

Give all three divs set dimensions and a white background colour. Also, position the cover and bg divs absolutely and apply a light grey border 1 pixel wide. Centre the container div on the page and place it 20 percent down from the top of the page:

```
.container, .cover, .bg {
    width:311px;
    height:138px;
    background-color:#fff;
}
.container {
    margin:20% auto 0 auto;
}
.cover, .bg {
    position:absolute;
    border:1px solid #aaa;
}
```

In addition, give the cover div a background image, which specifies what the cover actually looks like. Set the cursor to be the pointer graphic, and give it a z-index value of 3, because you want this div to be on top:

FIGURE 7.16 The covered video looks great.

```
.cover {
    background:#fff url('sintel-cover.jpg') no-repeat center center;
    z-index:3;
    cursor:pointer;
}
```

Now give the bg div a z-index, but a lower value of 2 so that the cover div will be stacked on top of it:

```
.bg {
    z-index:2;
}
```

Then simply give the video element a set dimension and a margin value of 5 pixels:

```
video {
    width:301px;
    height:128px;
    margin:5px;
}
```

Figure 7.16 shows how the video cover looks.

Of course, you now need to actually animate the cover, so that when a user clicks on it, it spins away and behind the video, revealing the video, which can then be played.

To implement the animation, you need to define the Keyframes function that will move the div and spin it at the same time. To achieve this, you'll use two different transforms, translate and rotate. The Keyframes function removecover is defined as:

```
@-moz-keyframes removecover {
    0% {
        -moz-transform:translate(0,0) rotate(0deg);
        z-index:3;
    }
    50% {
        -moz-transform:translate(-180px,-180px) rotate(-180deg);
        z-index:3;
    }
    100% {
        -moz-transform:translate(0,0) rotate(-360deg);
        z-index:1;
    }
}
```

NOTE: The animated cover example is defined for Firefox only using the -moz prefix. You can easily duplicate the rules for WebKit browsers by using the -webkit prefix instead.

Only three frames need to be defined here, because you want the div to move away to a certain point (-180 pixels away on the X and Y axes), rotate 360 degrees, and then return to the same position, but with one difference. Notice that the z-index is also specified within the frame definitions. Because the cover div will remain on top as it spins away and then settle behind the video and bg div, the z-index value defined in the final frame needs to be persisted once the animation is finished. You'll achieve this by using the animation-fill-mode property.

The animation definition is assigned to an animate class, which you will later assign to the cover div. The shorthand definition for the animation is:

```
div.animate {
    -moz-animation:removecover 2s 1 linear forwards;
}
```

So you assign the Keyframes removecover function to this animate class with a 2-second duration, iterate it once with a linear timing function, and set the animation-fill-mode to forwards so the rules contained in the final animation frame will persist once the animation is over—that is, a z-index of 1.

To ensure that the animation is smooth, add a transition to the cover div:

```
.cover {
    background:#fff url('sintel-cover.jpg') no-repeat center center;
    z-index:3;
    cursor:pointer;
    -moz-transition:all 1s ease;
    -webkit-transition:all 1s ease;
}
```

For the animation to actually happen, you simply add the CSS animate class to the cover div when the user clicks on it. Because you can't do this via CSS, a small bit of JavaScript is required to listen for the click event on the cover div and then append the class name:

```
var cover = document.querySelector('div.cover');
cover.addEventListener('click', function() {
    cover.className += ' animate';
}, false);
```

> **NOTE:** When appending to the element's class name, a space is also added before the new class name so that the element's class attribute maintains the required space-separated list of classes, for example, "cover animate".

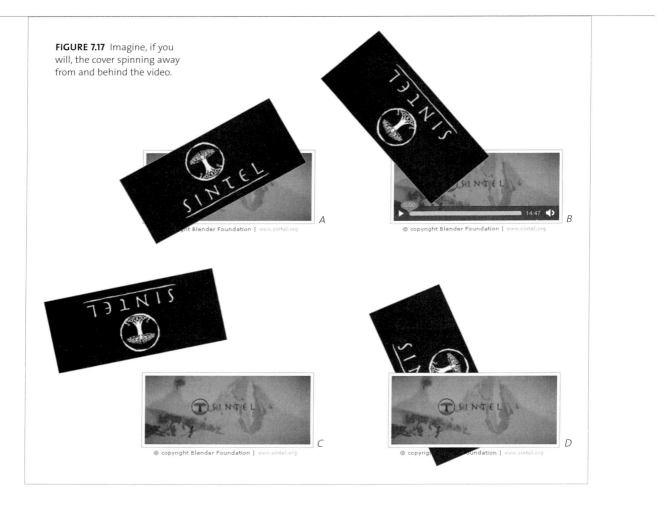

FIGURE 7.17 Imagine, if you will, the cover spinning away from and behind the video.

And that's it! When a user clicks on the cover, it will spin away from and behind the video, allowing the video to be played (**Figure 7.17**).

Let's now take a look at how you can use a 3D Transform in an animation.

ANIMATED SPIN

In the previous example, you combined CSS Transforms and Animation. Of course, it was a 2D Transform, but here you'll use a 3D Transform. This means that it only works on WebKit browsers, so the code will only target those browsers.

For this example, you'll use the rotate3d() transform mentioned earlier.

Once again, you first need to define the Keyframes function that will define the time frames for the animation. Using the whirring cogs of imagination, let's call this one spin:

```
@-webkit-keyframes spin {
    0% {
        -webkit-transform:rotate3d(0,0,0,0deg);
    }
    25% {
        -webkit-transform:rotate3d(0,1,0,90deg);
    }
    50% {
        -webkit-transform:rotate3d(0,1,0,180deg);
    }
    75% {
        -webkit-transform:rotate3d(0,1,0,240deg);
    }
    100% {
        -webkit-transform:rotate3d(0,1,0,360deg);
    }
}
```

FIGURE 7.18 A poor attempt at showing you a spinning video in Safari 5.1 through static images.

Again, you define five different time frames, each rotating the element on the Y axis at a different degree angle.

You then link up this function with the video's :hover state:

```
video:hover {
    -webkit-animation:spin 5s infinite linear;
}
```

And presto! It spins (**Figure 7.18**)!

Let's put what you've learned into practical use.

EXTENDING THE ANIMATED VIDEO COVER TO 3D

Using the animated video cover example you saw earlier, you can apply the rotate3d transform to the cover animation for WebKit browsers instead of the simpler rotate transform.

To do this, all you need to do is define the appropriate Keyframes animation removecover function for WebKit and assign it to the animate div class:

```
@-webkit-keyframes removecover {
    0% {
        -webkit-transform:translate(0,0) rotate3d(0,0,0,0deg);
        z-index:3;
    }
    50% {
        -webkit-transform:translate(-180px,-180px)
        → rotate3d(1,1,1,-180deg);
        z-index:3;
    }
    100% {
        -webkit-transform:translate(0,0) rotate3d(0,0,0,0deg);
        z-index:1;
    }
}
div.animate {
    -webkit-animation:removecover 2s 1 linear forwards;
}
```

FIGURE 7.19 Using that wonderful imagination of yours, watch the cover spin and rotate in 3D away from and behind the video!

Note that the 3D rotation is assigned to rotate around all three axes because it produces a better spinning effect when it's moving (**Figure 7.19**).

The information included in this section only dips into CSS Animations because an entire book could be written on them. But it does show you what you can do with animations and that anything you can do with them on other elements, you can also do to audio and video elements.

WRAPPING UP

CSS3 Transforms, Transitions, and Animations are powerful additions to the web developer's toolbox, and it's useful to know what they're capable of.

Even though browser support is currently sporadic, transitions and 2D Transforms are supported well enough for you to consider reading more about them, becoming familiar with them, and using them in your sites where appropriate. Moderation is key, so don't overdo them and overwhelm your users.

Most likely, it's only a matter of time before 3D Transforms and full animation are fully supported cross-browser, so keep an eye on their development as well.

Next, you'll move away from the world of styling and onto completely different but very useful features for HTML5 video in particular—video subtitling and other accessibility capabilities.

8

MULTIMEDIA AND ACCESSIBILITY

Up to now you've learned just how simple it can be to deliver audio and video across the Internet to your end users natively in HTML. Such power! But with this power comes responsibility.

You need to take a step back and think about your end users. Not all of them may be able to access the media as you intended. Some might have a sensory impairment; others might not understand the language your media is delivered in. What can you do to provide these users with access to the media you want to deliver?

In this chapter, you'll learn how HTML5 helps to provide you with several ways of presenting your media content to users. As a result, you'll increase the availability of your media to users with different needs and requirements, making it more accessible.

MEDIA AND POTENTIAL ACCESSIBILITY ISSUES

When thinking about the users who will be attempting to view your media content, you might make a number of assumptions:

- Users will view your content on a desktop, laptop, tablet, or phone.

- Users will have some way of listening to the audio of your content, be it via headphones or speakers.

- Users will be able to understand the language in which you deliver the media.

- Users will be able to successfully download and play your media.

All are fairly reasonable assumptions to make and most likely cover the vast majority of users who will want to access your content. You may be happy with your content being accessible to these users only; after all, majority rules, doesn't it?

Well, I'd strongly encourage you to think about making your content accessible to users who do not fall into the category of the assumptions just listed. Who are these viewers? They include:

- Users who have a sensory impairment that prevents them from listening to your content's audio or viewing video.

- Users who don't understand the language the media is delivered in.

- Users who use devices such as screen readers and/or use keyboards to access media content on the web.

- Users who can't successfully hear or view your content due to the environment they are in or because of device limitations.

Because most media content will usually include some audio, not being able to hear or understand the audio it contains is quite a showstopper in comprehending the content's message and information.

Equally, being able to access the content through a device such as a screen reader but then not being able to actually use it due to the media controls not being properly set up (e.g., for keyboard access) would annoy any user.

You'll explore the accessibility of media controls later in this chapter. You'll also take a look at what HTML5 brings to the table in an attempt to address the issue of users being unable to see, hear, or understand your media content. But first, let's take a quick look at what led to HTML5's attempt to confront this accessibility problem—SRT.

A **BRIEF LOOK** AT **SRT**

SRT is an existing file format for containing video subtitles and their timings. An SRT file is often produced automatically using a Windows program called SubRip (http://zuggy.wz.cz), which uses optical character recognition (OCR) to obtain the subtitles from the specified video source.

The SubRip file format is a basic text file with the .srt file extension that follows a basic format:

```
Subtitle number
hh:mm:ss,msmsms --> hh:mm:ss,msmsms
Subtitle Text (one or more lines)

...
```

Each subtitle set begins with a unique subtitle number, followed by the start and end timestamps of the timing the subtitle represents on a separate line, which is then followed by one or more lines of subtitle text. Each subsequent subtitle set is separated by a blank line. The timestamp format hh:mm:ss,msmsms specifies the hours, minutes, seconds, and milliseconds of the time in question. Note that the millisecond separator is a comma.

An example of such a file follows:

```
1
00:00:10,500 --> 00:00:13,000
Elephant's Dream

2
00:00:15,000 --> 00:00:18,000
At the left we can see...
```

The SRT file format is quite popular and is often the format that video subtitles are released in. This file format isn't currently used as part of HTML5's attempt to tackle accessibility, although it was to begin with but has now been extended and given a new name, WebVTT.

INTRODUCING **WEBVTT**

WebVTT (Web Video Text Tracks) is a file format that is intended for marking up external text tracks. It was initially part of the WHATWG and the W3C HTML5 specifications, and was an extension of SRT called WebSRT (Web Subtitle Resource Tracks). But the W3C was concerned that HTML5 should be independent of any chosen captioning format, and therefore, it was removed from that specification.

NOTE: Even though the SRT in WebSRT stands for Subtitle Resource Tracks, the original acronym didn't stand for anything and merely reflected the file extension used. WebSRT is a "backronym"; Subtitle Resource Tracks was shoe-horned into the three letters to actually mean something.

The presence of WebVTT is currently one major difference between the WHATWG HTML5 specification and the W3C specification.

Although no browser currently supports WebVTT, major browser vendors have indicated that they will implement support for WebVTT in the future. This indication has led to the creation of a WebVTT Working Group Charter (www.w3.org/2011/05/google-webvtt-charter.html) at the W3C, whose mission is to:

> "create a W3C specification starting from the WHATWG WebVTT (Web Video Text Tracks) language and solidify it through the creation of a WebVTT test suite and through the creation of semantic mappings of other subtitle formats to or from WebVTT in order to facilitate browser implementation and market adoption."

This promise of vendor support will hopefully in turn eventually lead to a formal standardisation of the WebVTT specification at the W3C. With browser support and that of the W3C, you can be sure that WebVTT is here to stay and is destined become the de facto method of marking up text tracks within audio and video content on the web.

So what is the WebVTT file format and how can it help you make your content accessible? Read on.

WHAT CAN WEBVTT DO?

You use the WebVTT file format to define WebVTT files. One of the main uses of these files is to provide subtitles to video content, although the format of the file doesn't indicate what its contents are used for.

The WebVTT format also allows you to provide a textual description of the video content, which can then be used by various accessibility devices (which might read the descriptions out loud) to describe the content of the video to those who cannot see it. You inform the browser of the WebVTT file and of its purpose using HTML markup; you'll find out how this is done later in this chapter when you read about the track element.

Let's take a look at the WebVTT file format in more detail.

WEBVTT FILE FORMAT

A WebVTT file is a simple text file with the .vtt extension that needs to follow a specified format, which you will look at shortly. The file must be encoded as UTF-8 and labeled with the MIME type text/tt. The line terminators within the file can only be \r (a carriage return), \n (a new line), or \r\n (a carriage return followed by a new line). It must also contain a WebVTT file body, which consists of the following:

```
WEBVTT

[cue]

[cue]
...
```

The WEBVTT string at the top identifies the contents as a WebVTT file and must then be followed by at least one blank line, which is then followed by any number of cues, each of which is separated by a blank line.

A cue is defined as:

```
[idstring]
[hh:]mm:ss.msmsms --> [hh:]mm:ss.msmsms [cue settings]
TextLine1
TextLine2
...
```

idstring is a unique identifier within the file that identifies the cue. It can consist of one or more characters that do not contain the substring "-->" or any of the line terminators mentioned earlier.

`[hh:]mm:ss.msmsms --> [hh:]mm:ss.msmsms` indicates the timestamp range within the video file that the cue is specified for. `[hh:]mm:ss.msmsms` is a simple timestamp; the hour portion is optional (depending on the length of the video in question of course).

NOTE: The millisecond separators are full stops, not commas as in SRT.

`cue settings` allow you to specify the positioning of the text; you'll read more about them in a moment.

`TextLineN` is the actual text in the video file that the timestamp range in the cue represents. The content can be all in one line or presented in any number of separate lines. Any lines will be contained within the cue until a blank line is encountered, which indicates the end of that particular cue.

Let's take a quick look at a sample WebVTT file containing two timestamp ranges:

```
WEBVTT

1
00:00:10.500 --> 00:00:13.000
Elephant's Dream

2
00:00:15.000 --> 00:00:18.000
At the left we can see...
```

This example defines two cues: The first one starts 10 seconds and 500 milliseconds into the video and ends at 13 seconds in, and the second one starts 15 seconds into the video and ends 3 seconds later. The subtitle text for each cue is given below its timestamp.

Using cues is relatively straightforward, and you can see how the file can be built up with a number of cues to cover the length of an entire video. You can also specify some settings on a per-cue basis. These affect the positioning of the cue on

FIGURE 8.1 How a subtitle cue might appear on a video with no cue settings specified.

the related video. You can have a number of setting values, and a cue setting can contain one or more values, each one separated by a space. The various settings are listed in **Table 8.1**.

If no cue settings are specified, the text will align to the middle, at the bottom of the video frame (**Figure 8.1**).

TABLE 8.1 WebVTT Cue Settings

MEANING	FORMAT	VALUES	EFFECT
Text direction	D:value	vertical	Vertical right to left.
		vertical-lr	Vertical left to right.
Line position	L:value	0–100%	Percentage position of the cue relative to the video frame.
		[–]number	Line number to be displayed on.
Text alignment	A:value	start	Text aligned to start of the line.
		middle	Text aligned to middle of the line.
		end	Text aligned to end of the line.
Text position	T:value	0-100%	Percentage position of cue text relative to the video frame.
Text size	S:value	0-100%	The percentage size of the cue text.

FIGURE 8.2 How a cue subtitle might appear on a video with a cue setting of `A:start`.

Elephant's Dream

Let's add some of these settings to the example used earlier:

```
WEBVTT

1
00:00:10.500 --> 00:00:13.000 A:start
Elephant's Dream

2
00:00:15.000 --> 00:00:18.000 A:end L:10%
At the left we can see...
```

The text in the first cue will be aligned to the left of the video (much the same way as the CSS rule `text-align:left` works) (**Figure 8.2**).

The second cue has two settings applied to it: The text will be aligned to the end of the line (similar to `text-align:right` in CSS) and will be placed on the line 10 percent down from the top of the video (**Figure 8.3**).

In addition to specifying cue settings for controlling the positioning and alignment of cue text, there are also a number of inline styles that you can apply to the text. These look and act the same as HTML elements. They contain a start and an end tag, and the formatting is applied to the text in between. These tags are listed in **Table 8.2**.

FIGURE 8.3 How a cue subtitle might appear on a video with a cue setting of `A:end L:10%`.

TABLE 8.2 WebVTT Text Tags

TAG NAME	DESCRIPTION
c	Defines class text that permits a CSS style class name to be added to the tag, e.g., `<c.className>`.
i	Italicises the text content.
b	Bolds the text content.
u	Underlines the text content.
v	Defines voice content that permits a voice name to be added to the tag, e.g., `<v.Speaker1>`, which can then be styled via CSS.
ruby	Defines ruby content (short runs of text alongside base text, often used in East Asian documents to indicate pronunciation or to provide short annotations. See www.w3.org/TR/css3-ruby for further information).
`[hh:]mm:ss.msmsms`	Defines a timestamp at which a certain piece of content within the cue text becomes active. Similar to karaoke-style text, appearing step by step. Note that there is no end tag; the text after the timestamp will appear unless it encounters another timestamp or it's the end of the cue.

Let's extend the example further and use some of the text tags to format the cue text:

FIGURE 8.4 Video-cue text with a style defined using CSS and the WebVTT c text tag.

```
WEBVTT

1
00:00:00.000 --> 00:00:14.999
Elephant's <c.dream>Dream</c>

2
00:00:15.000 --> 00:00:18.000 A:end L:10%
At the <i>left</i> we can <b>see</b> ...

3
00:00:18.167 --> 00:00:22.000
At the right <00:00:20.000>we can see the...
```

With the first cue, a class name of "dream" has been added, a style for which you can define within your HTML file in the same way as you'd create any CSS style rules. In **Figure 8.4**, the "dream" CSS class has been defined with red text and uppercase text.

NOTE: Any CSS class names that you might use within your WebVTT subtitle definitions can be defined in the containing HTML file or an external CSS file in the same way as you'd specify any other CSS classes.

FIGURE 8.5 Video-cue text that uses the i and b text tags.

FIGURE 8.6 This video-cue text shows the text in stages.

The second cue now has tags that will display the word "left" in italics and "see" in bold type (**Figure 8.5**).

An extra cue is added to this example to show how the timestamp is used to display the text "karaoke style." When the cue starts, the words "At the right" will appear first. Then the text "we can see..." will be displayed at the appropriate time-stamp (**Figure 8.6**).

NOTE: If you want the characters &, <, and > to appear in the text of a video cue, you need to escape them with & < and > respectively.

WEBVTT FUTURE DEVELOPMENTS

It's worth noting that because the WebVTT file format is relatively new to the specification and with the recent creation of the WebVTT Working Group Charter, additions to the specification are likely.

If you want to keep abreast of any changes to this specification, keep an eye on the Working Group Charter's site (www.w3.org/2011/05/google-webvtt -charter.html) and the blog of Silvia Pfeiffer (http://blog.gingertech.net) who is currently editor of the Working Group Charter. Silvia also blogs regularly about HTML5-related accessibility topics.

You can see how the complete narrative in a video could be added to a WebVTT text file with formatting and styling.

But how do you connect a WebVTT file with a particular video? This is where the new HTML5 track element steps in.

THE **TRACK** ELEMENT

The track element is one of the new HTML5 elements. Its purpose is to allow external text tracks to be specified for media elements, such as audio and video. The track element does not represent anything on its own and must be used in conjunction with, and as a child of, a media element.

The track element takes a number of attributes, which are listed in **Table 8.3**.

TABLE 8.3 Track Element Attributes

ATTRIBUTE	DESCRIPTION
src	Contains the URL to the text track data (e.g., a WebVTT file).
kind	Defines the type of content the track definition (and the source defined in src) is to be used for. It can have a number of values: • subtitles. A transcription or translation of the media element's dialog; suitable for when the audio is available to the user but not understood. • captions. Similar to subtitles, but also contains sound effects, music cues, and other relevant audio information; suitable for when the soundtrack is unavailable to the user. • descriptions. Textual descriptions of the video component of the media resource; suitable for when the visual component is unavailable. • chapters. Chapter titles intended for navigating the media resource. This could be displayed to users for them to choose from a list to jump to the appropriately named chapter in the video. • metadata. Tracks intended for use from script. The browser will usually not display them to the user. This data could be used by devices to determine such things as whether it can display it or not.
srclang	Specifies the language that the text track data pointed to in src is in. Must be present if kind is set to subtitles.
label	Provides a user-readable title for the track, which can be displayed to users when they are asked to choose between, for example, English or German subtitles.
default	If this attribute is present, it indicates that this track is the one to be used as the default if the user does not indicate a preference.
ruby	Defines ruby content (short runs of text alongside base text, often used in East Asian documents to indicate pronunciation or to provide short annotations. See www.w3.org/TR/css3-ruby for further information).
[hh:]mm:ss. msmsms	Defines a timestamp at which a certain piece of content within the cue text becomes active. Similar to karaoke-style text, appearing step by step. Note that there is no end tag; the text after the timestamp will appear unless it encounters another timestamp or it's the end of the cue.

The following example shows how a `track` element might be used in connection with a video to provide subtitles:

```
<video controls>
    <source src="video-file.mp4" type="video/mp4">
    <source src="video-file.webm" type="video/webm">
    <track src="en.vtt" kind="subtitles" srclang="en" label="English
    → subtitles">
</video>
```

The `track` element in the example specifies that the `en.vtt` file contains English subtitles (as the `label` says) in the English language (`srclang` is set to en) of kind: `subtitles` for the surrounding `video` element. From this example, you can see just how easy it would be to add a second subtitles file that might be in a different language:

```
<video controls>
    <source src="video-file.mp4" type="video/mp4">
    <source src="video-file.webm" type="video/webm">
    <track src="en.vtt" kind="subtitles" srclang="en" label="English
    → subtitles" default>
    <track src="de.vtt" kind="subtitles" srclang="de" label="German
    → subtitles">
</video>
```

Here, another `track` definition has been added, pointing to a `de.vtt` file that contains German subtitles; `srclang` is set to de.

Notice that the `default` attribute has been added to the English subtitles definition, marking it as the default subtitle set to be used if the user doesn't specifically select one.

If you wanted to extend the example further and add a chapter listing in each language (English and German), you would do the following:

```
<video controls>
    <source src="video-file.mp4" type="video/mp4">
    <source src="video-file.webm" type="video/webm">
    <track src="en.vtt" kind="subtitles" srclang="en" label="English
    ⇥ subtitles" default>
    <track src="de.vtt" kind="subtitles" srclang="de" label="German
    ⇥ subtitles">
    <track src="ch-en.vtt" kind="chapters" srclang="en"
    ⇥ label="English chapter listing" default>
    <track src="ch-de.vtt" kind="chapters" srclang="de"
    ⇥ label="German chapter listing">
</video>
```

Once the various WebVTT files have been created with the content you want, it's a fairly simple process to add them to the appropriate video.

Everything you've just read about WebVTT all sounds quite promising; however, even though some browsers support the track element to some degree, currently no browser supports the WebVTT file format.

NOTE: At the time of this writing, the WebKit (which Chrome and Safari are based on) nightly build has some support for WebVTT.

All is not lost, though, because several JavaScript libraries are available that enable you to start using WebVTT today.

USING **WEBVTT** AND THE **TRACK ELEMENT** NOW

A small number of browsers support the track element to some degree. The latest WebKit browsers (e.g., Chrome 12 and Safari 5.0.5) recognise the element but don't do anything with it. The current version of Firefox (5) parses the element but also does nothing with it. Although these browsers are taking steps in the right direction, they don't really help you implement WebVTT now.

Fortunately, four JavaScript libraries allow you to define the track element with WebVTT files in your web document that will deliver what you want:

- **Playr.** http://www.delphiki.com/html5/playr
  Supports: subtitles, chapters, some cue settings
  Browsers: Opera, Chrome, Safari, Firefox

- **LeanBack Player.** http://dev.mennerich.name/showroom/html5_video
  Supports: subtitles
  Browsers: All major browsers with fallback to Flash if required

- **Captionator.** https://github.com/cgiffard/Captionator
  (CaptionCrunch version)
  Supports: subtitles, all cue settings
  Browsers: Opera, Chrome, Safari, Firefox, IE9

- **MediaElementJS.** http://mediaelementjs.com
  Supports: subtitles (timing format uses SRT format)
  Browsers: All major browsers with fallback to Flash if required

---

SRT SUPPORT

Although only a handful of JavaScript players support WebVTT, a number of them support SRT subtitle files. Those players that support WebVTT (Playr, LeanBack, Captionator, and MediaElementJS) also support SRT in addition to the following that provide support for SRT only:

- **js_videosub.** https://bitbucket.org/tagawa/jscaptions

- **jscaptions.** http://www.storiesinflight.com/js_videosub

- **Kaltura.** http://www.kaltura.org/project/HTML5_Video_Media_JavaScript_Library

None of these libraries offer support for all the different values for the kind attribute of the track element: They only support the subtitle value (Playr also supports the chapter value). Because subtitles are one of the most important values, it's a good start. This support also allows you to begin adding subtitles to your videos now and seeing them in action.

Let's look at how you might use the Playr JavaScript library to add subtitles and chapters to a video.

PLAYR EXAMPLE

To use Playr, you must first download it from the Playr download website at https://github.com/delphiki/Playr. Once downloaded, you need to include the Playr CSS file and JavaScript in your web document:

```
<link rel="stylesheet" href="playr.css" />
<script src="playr.js"></script>
```

When defining your video, you simply add the CSS class "playr_video" to your video element, and Playr will automatically be used for that video.

A sample of Playr with a short animated film called Elephant's Dream (© copyright 2006, Blender Foundation, Netherlands Media Art Institute, www.elephantsdream.org) is available on the book's website at www.html5multimedia.com.

The code used for this video is as follows:

```
<video class="playr_video" preload="metadata" controls
→  poster="elephants-dream.title.jpg">

   <source src="elephants-dream-medium.mp4" type="video/mp4">

   <source src="elephants-dream-medium.webm" type="video/webm">

   <track label="English subtitles" kind="subtitles" srclang="en"
   →  src="elephants-dream-subtitles-en.vtt" default>

   <track label="German subtitles" kind="subtitles" srclang="de"
   →  src="elephants-dream-subtitles-de.vtt">

   <track label="Chapters" kind="chapters" srclang="en"
   →  src="elephants-dream-chapters-en.vtt">

</video>
```

FIGURE 8.7 The Playr video player with Elephant's Dream.

Figure 8.7 shows how this video and track definition would look in the Playr video player.

Also, three `track` elements are used to point to English and German subtitles, and English chapters.

NOTE: Playr currently doesn't support multiple chapter files or the `default` attribute but will do so in a future release.

Figures 8.8 through **8.11** show how Playr displays the different options.

Playr is a handy video player, and its ability to display subtitles and chapters is very useful. Support for the other kinds of `track` element contents are planned, so like other available video players, it will keep on improving.

Another important part of making media content accessible are the controls. Next, you'll learn how accessible the default players are and what can you do to make your own custom controls more accessible.

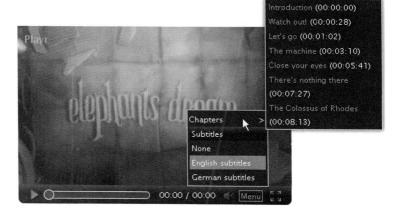

FIGURE 8.8 Playr's menu allows viewers to choose English and German subtitles plus chapters.

FIGURE 8.9 Subtitles have been placed 6 percent from the top (using L:6%) and bolded with <b>.

FIGURE 8.10 The same video with German subtitles chosen.

FIGURE 8.11 A sample of how chapter selection looks in Playr.

MEDIA CONTROLS AND ACCESSIBILITY

As mentioned earlier, it's quite important for accessibility that the media controls can be accessed from the keyboard. Browsers have their own set of controls for media elements, but how accessible are they from the keyboard? Unfortunately, at the moment, the answer is not very. Opera seems to be the only browser whose default control set is immediately accessible from the keyboard. You can easily tab from one control to the other, use the Return key to toggle the Play/Pause button, and use the arrow keys to control the seek bar and volume control.

So, if you want to make your media content fully accessible across all modern browsers, you need to implement your own custom controls. In Chapter 5, you learned how to add custom controls, and it is these custom controls that you will now extend to make them more accessible.

IMPROVING THE ACCESSIBILITY OF CUSTOM CONTROLS

You've already used the HTML button element to implement nearly all of the controls. Using button elements immediately increases the accessibility of the controls because the button element is automatically accessible from the keyboard. That fact alone makes the custom controls keyboard accessible. Because the controls are also listed in the same order as they appear on the player, their tab order is also pretty much in the required logical order. However, you might want to change the tab order of the progress bar and the Play/Pause button. Most likely, users would want to play the video first, so that button should be the first control that they can access.

You can specify the tab order of HTML controls using the tabindex attribute. The order specified by this attribute is the one that the browser will tell the keyboard to follow. So you apply a tabindex of 1 to the Play/Pause button and 2 to the progress bar, and then apply subsequent tabindexes in the order in which they appear in the source:

```
<div id="controls">

    <div id="progressBar"><span id="played" tabindex="2"></span>
    → </div>

    <button id="playpause" alt="play" title="play" tabindex="1">
    → play</button>

    <button id="stop" alt="stop" title="stop" tabindex="3">stop
    → </button>

    <button id="rewind" alt="rewind" title="rewind" tabindex="4">
    → &laquo;</button>

    <button id="ffwd" alt="fast forward" title="fast forward"
    → tabindex="5">&raquo;</button>

    <button id="volumeDown" alt="decrease volume" title="-"
    → tabindex="6">button</button>

    <button id="volumeUp" alt="increase volume" title="+"
    → tabindex="7">+</button>

    <button id="mute" alt="mute" title="mute" tabindex="8">mute
    → </button>

</div>
```

NOTE: In this code listing, the `onclick()` events have been omitted for brevity.

THE **RANGE** ELEMENT

In Chapter 5, it was mentioned that the HTML5 range element wasn't used in the custom media control set due to its limited support across HTML5 browsers.

The range element would be ideal for use as a progress bar if support was better because it too automatically provides keyboard accessibility, and the seek bar would work via the keyboard (the up and down keys would toggle the seek when the element has focus) without any further requirements.

Because the buttons provide keyboard accessibility automatically, all you need to tackle now is the progress bar, which uses a div and a span.

Just as in Chapter 5, you need to add an event listener for the keypress event, which fires when a key is pressed, and then act on it. You're interested in just a key press on the progress bar, so the event is added to the progress bar only:

```
var progressBar = document.getElementById("progressBar");
progressBar.addEventListener("keypress", function(e) {
    checkKey(e.keyCode);
}, false);
```

The function that is called when a key press is detected is called checkKey() with a parameter indicating the numeric code of the key that was pressed:

```
function checkKey(code) {
    if (code == 38) { // up arrow key
        video.currentTime += 0.5;
    }
    else if (code == 40) { // down arrow key
        video.currentTime -= 0.5;
    }
}
```

The checkKey() function simply checks the key code to see if it's the up arrow key (code 38) or the down arrow key (code 40). Depending on which key it is, the video's currentTime attribute is increased or decreased by 0.05 (an arbitrary time value, but it seems a good step to move the video forward or backward by).

And that's it. The progress bar's seek capabilities can now be accessed via the keyboard with the up and down arrow keys when it's in focus. The end result renders your media custom controls a lot more accessible than they would have been.

WRAPPING UP

With regard to accessibility, HTML5 has advanced and expanded from its initial definition of the WebSRT file format to WebVTT. With browser vendors planning to support this format, a new W3C Working Group was formed with the intention of formalising the WebVTT specification for browsers to start supporting. So hopefully, browser support is only a matter of time.

Although native support is currently patchy, you can use existing JavaScript libraries to add subtitles to your videos now. These libraries will undoubtedly increase their functionality and capabilities in the future.

You can also make the custom media controls you built in Chapter 5 more accessible via the keyboard.

Overall, accessibility is a goal you should be thinking about when serving multimedia content to your users. The more users who can access your content the better, right?

The next chapter moves away from accessibility and explores how HTML5 multimedia can interact with one of the more exciting HTML5 features, canvas.

9

USING **VIDEO** WITH **CANVAS**

In addition to native multimedia, one of the most talked about capabilities that HTML5 brings to the web table is the ability to draw and manipulate graphics using JavaScript via the new canvas element. The canvas element defines an area on a web page that you can draw on using a JavaScript API.

Canvas and its corresponding API have many uses, from copying media and drawing simple graphs to filling colours, directly manipulating pixels, and creating complex games that are played inside the browser without needing a third-party plugin.

You can also use multimedia elements in interactions with canvas and the API. This chapter briefly explores some of these simple interactions, with, as always, fully explained examples.

THE **CANVAS** ELEMENT

The brief chapter introduction told you what you can use the canvas element for and that it's actually quite useless on its own. However, it is very easy to use and only has two possible attributes, which are listed in **Table 9.1**.

TABLE 9.1 Canvas Element Attributes

ATTRIBUTE	DESCRIPTION
width	Defines the width of the canvas drawing area.
height	Defines the height of the canvas drawing area.

That's it, really! You can, of course, also define the canvas's dimensions using CSS or JavaScript. And just like every other HTML element, the position, borders, and so on of the canvas element can be defined via CSS.

Defining a canvas element on your web document is as simple as this:

```
<canvas width="500" height="500"></canvas>
```

TIP: You should always specify the width and height of your canvas element using the attributes, CSS, or JavaScript. If you don't, the element's dimensions will default to 300×150 pixels.

Of course, leaving it at that renders absolutely nothing of interest on the web page, so you probably wouldn't see a thing because it would render as a blank space. You could add a border to it via CSS so you could actually view it when you are experimenting.

The canvas is a two-dimensional grid, and as such has two axes, X and Y. To define a position within the canvas, you specify two coordinates on this grid (X, Y). The top-left corner position of the grid is considered "home" and has the coordinates $(0,0)$.

BROWSER SUPPORT

Browser support for the canvas element and the accompanying API are rather good—all major browsers support them. Internet Explorer 8 and earlier versions, of course, do not support them, but you can use Google's ExplorerCanvas JavaScript library (http://code.google.com/p/explorercanvas) to bring canvas and API support to those browsers.

But to actually do anything useful with the canvas element, you need to invoke the 2D JavaScript API, which is what you'll do next.

THE **2D API**

Although the canvas element is part of the HTML5 specification, the 2D API that you use to draw on it was, but is no longer, part of the specification. It was moved into its own specification at the W3C (http://dev.w3.org/html5/2dcontext).

The 2D API has a whole host of different functions and functionality, which are beyond the scope of this chapter. However, you'll learn about and use a few of these functions in the examples throughout the chapter. You are, of course, encouraged to seek out one (or more) of the many books on the subject.

The canvas contains a drawing context, which is where the actual drawing takes place. At the moment, only a 2D context exists, but the HTML5 specification mentions that it's likely there will be a 3D context available in the future (no date is given of course!).

To use the 2D drawing context, you need to get a handle to it. But first you need to get a handle to the canvas element, which is easily done using one of the standard JavaScript functions querySelector() or getElementById():

```
var canvas = document.querySelector('canvas');
```

To get a handle on the 2D drawing context, you use the getContext() function, which accepts one argument and at the moment can only have the value 2d.

```
var context = canvas.getContext('2d');
```

And there you have your context handle, which you can use to draw on the canvas. You'll do that next using the fillRect() function.

The fillRect(x, y, w, h) function draws a simple rectangle on the canvas, and it takes four arguments: the X and Y coordinates where the rectangle is to be placed (its top-left corner), and the width and height of the rectangle.

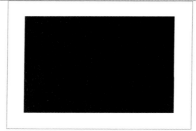

FIGURE 9.1 A simple rectangle drawn on the canvas element using the `fillRect()` function.

The following code draws a black (the default colour) rectangle that is 150 × 100 pixels at the X and Y coordinates (20,20):

```
context.fillRect(20, 20, 150, 100);
```

Figure 9.1 shows the resulting rectangle.

The `fillRect()` function is one of the most basic functions of the 2D API, and you'll use it quite often. Other functions allow you to draw lines and circles, but because you don't need them for the main examples that follow, they aren't discussed here.

TIP: For a good grounding in HTML5 canvas basics, check out http://dev.opera.com/articles/view/html-5-canvas-the-basics.

Now that you have an understanding of the canvas element and a basic understanding of the 2D API, let's move on to an example that allows you to take screen shots of an HTML5 video.

TAKING A **SCREEN SHOT**
OF AN **HTML5 VIDEO**

Say, for example, that you want to allow users to take screen shots of your video as it's playing and display them somewhere else, for example, on the web page next to the video. You can use a canvas element as the drawing surface in which to actually place the screen shot image.

Sound a bit complicated? Well, it's not. You only need to use two of the JavaScript API functions: fillRect()and one other that you'll read about in a moment.

Before you take the screen shot, you must first set up the video and a button for taking the screen shot, as well as complete a few other initialisation tasks.

First up, set up the HTML for the video, button, and canvas elements:

```
<video controls>
    <source src="elephants-dream-medium.mp4" type="video/mp4">
    <source src="elephants-dream-medium.webm" type="video/webm">
</video>
<canvas></canvas>
<button id="snap">Take screenshot</button>
```

Notice that there's no width and height specified on the canvas element yet; that will be done via JavaScript later, so don't worry! You'll also add a function to the onclick event of the button element; again, this will happen a bit later on.

Now on to some JavaScript. Recall that you need to grab a handle to the 2D drawing context of the canvas element. You also need to get a handle to the video element because you'll need that later:

```
var video = document.querySelector('video');
var canvas = document.querySelector('canvas');
var context = canvas.getContext('2d');
var w, h, ratio;
```

Some other variables are also defined for later use: for example, the w (width) and h (height), whose names make the data they'll contain quite obvious.

In this example, you'll create screen shots that are smaller than the video. This shows that it is possible to work with screen shots that have a different size than the original video.

It was mentioned earlier that the dimensions of the canvas element need to be defined should you want to override the default dimensions of 300 × 150, which you do here. Therefore, you need to work out the ratio of the video's width to its height (hence the ratio variable defined in the previous code snippet). You also can only do this when the video is actually available for the browser to be able to check the dimensions of the video. So, you need to wait until the video's dimensions are available. And how do you do this? By listening for the loadedmetadata API event that you may recall from Chapter 5:

```
video.addEventListener('loadedmetadata', function() {
    ratio = video.videoWidth / video.videoHeight;
    w = video.videoWidth - 100;
    h = parseInt(w / ratio, 10);
    canvas.width = w;
    canvas.height = h;
}, false);
```

When the loadedmetadata event is raised, the ratio of the video is calculated. The w variable is then set to be (arbitrarily) 100 less than the actual width of the video, and the h variable is set to whatever ratio the value in w is to the video's ratio. The canvas element's width and height are then set to the calculated values in w and h.

You then need to define the actual function that will take the screen shot and attach it to the button's onclick event. But before you do so, let's take a quick look at the other 2D API function that you'll need here, drawImage().

The drawImage(image, x, y, w, h) function can take a number of parameters, but you'll only use five of them in this example. As its name suggests, this function allows you to draw an image onto the canvas. The first parameter is the image to draw, and the next four are the same as in fillRect(): the X and Y coordinates of the drawn image's top-left corner, and its width and height.

TIP: For more information on the drawImage() function and the various parameters it can take, see www.whatwg.org/specs/web-apps/current-work/multipage/the-canvas-element.html#drawimage.

The image parameter can be one of the following HTML elements: img, canvas, or video. Yes, the video element can be passed to this function, and it will automatically create an image from the current frame of the video in question and draw it on the canvas.

Next, you define the function snap() to take the actual screen shot and attach it to the button element:

```
<button id="snap" onclick="snap()">Take screenshot</button>
```

And snap() is defined as:

```
function snap() {
    context.fillRect(0, 0, w, h);
    context.drawImage(video, 0, 0, w, h);
}
```

Two lines are all that are required! The rectangle in the canvas that will be filled is defined first—in this case it's the entire canvas element—and then you use drawImage() to draw the image from the video.

TIP: You can clear whatever is in a canvas element by simply redefining the width and height of the canvas, which effectively resets it.

FIGURE 9.2 The canvas element on the right (A) is empty to begin with until the "Take screenshot" button is clicked, which draws a still from the video as an image on the canvas (B).

That's all it takes to take a screen shot from the video. As the video is playing, you can keep clicking the "Take screenshot" button and a new screen shot of the video will be taken at whatever point it's at (**Figure 9.2**).

Most of the coding effort involved setting up the video, button, and canvas elements, whereas the actual work only took two lines, which is the biggest advantage of canvas and is kinda cool.

You'll expand on this example next by copying the entire video into the canvas element as it's playing.

In the previous example, you saw how easy it was to take screen shots of a video as it's playing. But what if you wanted to take that a bit further and update the copied image automatically as the main video is playing, in effect, creating an exact copy of the video, but smaller? All you need to do is use the same code from the preceding example and add listeners for various events that update the image in the canvas element.

Recall from Chapter 5 the events that are raised when a video is playing, paused, stopped, or ended. It is these events, more specifically the play, paused, and ended events, that you need to use.

To achieve the video copy, you need to use the standard setInterval() function, which allows you to specify that a particular JavaScript function is to be called at specific intervals. When the video starts to play, you listen and catch the play event, and using the setInterval() function, set the snap() function you defined earlier to be called every 33 milliseconds:

```
video.addEventListener('play', function() {
    setInterval("snap()", 33);
}, false);
```

FIGURE 9.3 The canvas element on the right updates automatically as the video is playing, keeping it in sync with the video (A and B).

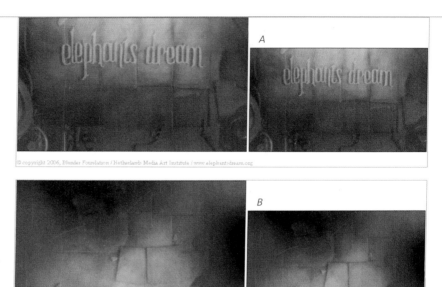

This code causes the snap() function to automatically update the canvas's drawing context with a new screen shot of the video, which makes it look like it's actually playing (**Figure 9.3**).

You also should listen for when the video has been paused or ended (using the paused and ended events) so that you can stop the snap() function from being called at the intervals defined. To clear an interval, you call the standard JavaScript function clearInterval():

```
video.addEventListener('paused', function() {
    clearInterval();
}, false);
video.addEventListener('ended', function() {
    clearInterval();
}, false);
```

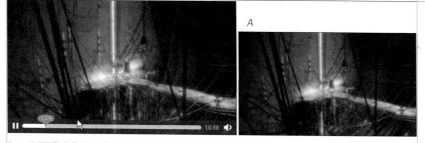

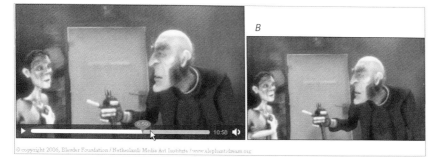

FIGURE 9.4 The video stays in sync (A) even when you use the seek control to jump ahead in the video (B).

And that's all there is to it. When you play the video, it will update the image in the canvas as it's playing, even if you skip ahead (**Figure 9.4**). And when you pause it or end it, the canvas image will stop being updated.

In a similar vein, but slightly more complicated, you'll next make the video copy appear in greyscale, unlike the colour original. To do this, you need to manipulate the actual pixels of the video, which once again is not as complicated as it might sound.

Another useful thing that you can do with objects within the canvas drawing context is to alter the individual pixels. You'll do just that in this example by altering the pixels in the video so they appear grey rather than in colour.

You'll be building on the code created in the first example in this chapter. So, the first thing you need to do is to define a second canvas for the manipulations to take place. This is used as a background canvas, which you'll use to work on before drawing the final result on the actual display canvas. The background canvas will only exist within the JavaScript code, not as an HTML element on the page, and therefore won't be seen by the user.

To do this, you simply create a new instance of the canvas element using the standard createElement() JavaScript function:

```
var bgCanvas= document.createElement('canvas');
```

Once this instance has been created, you also need a handle to its 2D drawing context so you can use it:

```
var bgContext = bgCanvas.getContext('2d');
```

In the earlier example, you set the width and height of the display canvas via JavaScript, and you also need to set the background canvas to the same dimensions:

```
video.addEventListener('loadedmetadata', function() {
    ratio = video.videoWidth / video.videoHeight;
    w = video.videoWidth - 100;
    h = parseInt(w / ratio, 10);
    canvas.width = w;
    canvas.height = h;
    bgCanvas.width = w;
    bgCanvas.height = h;
}, false);
```

Before you alter the pixels, you need to meet two new functions that you'll use: getImageData(x, y, w, h) and putImageData(imageData, x, y). The getImageData(x, y, w, h) function returns an ImageData object for the rectangle specified by the parameters: x and y specify the upper-left corner of the rectangle, and w and h are the rectangle's width and height.

The ImageData object that is returned, as its name suggests, contains the image data for the rectangle specified in the call getImageData(). The information that this returned object contains is listed in **Table 9.2**.

TABLE 9.2 ImageData Object Contents

ATTRIBUTE	DESCRIPTION
width	The width of the returned image data rectangle.
height	The height of the returned image data rectangle.
data	A two-dimensional array that contains the actual pixel information for each pixel. Each pixel has four entries listed sequentially; values for the pixels are red, green, blue, and alpha channel.
	For example, if the first pixel is white, it would contain the information:

	`data[0][0] = 255  // red channel`
	`data[0][1] = 255  // green channel`
	`data[0][2] = 255  // blue channel`
	`data[0][3] = 1    // alpha channel (opacity)`

As you've probably guessed, it will be through the data attribute that you'll be able to alter the pixel information of the image.

The other function, putImageData(imageData, x, y), paints the pixel data specified in imageData at the coordinates indicated by x and y. Using this information, let's make the video grey!

Define the function `makeItGrey()`, which will do all the required shenanigans:

```
function makeItGrey() {
    bgContext.drawImage(video, 0, 0, w, h);
    var pixelData = bgContext.getImageData(0, 0, w, h);
    for (var i = 0; i < pixelData.data.length; i += 4 ) {
        var r = pixelData.data[i];
        var g = pixelData.data[i+1];
        var b = pixelData.data[i+2];
        var averageColour = (r + g + b) / 3;
        pixelData.data[i] = averageColour;
        pixelData.data[i+1] = averageColour;
        pixelData.data[i+2] = averageColour;
    }
    context.putImageData(pixelData, 0, 0);
}
```

Let's walk through the code, starting with the background context:

```
bgContext.drawImage(video, 0, 0, w, h);
```

Similar to the earlier example, you need to take a snapshot of the video and draw it to the canvas. You do the same here, but this time you draw the image on the background context rather than the display context.

You then obtain the pixel data from the background context's image that you've just drawn. You'll be manipulating the data returned in the `pixelData` object:

```
var pixelData = bgContext.getImageData(0, 0, w, h);
```

You then need to loop through each item in the `pixelData`s data array, which contains the actual information for each pixel. As mentioned in Table 9.2, the data array is a two-dimensional array with four data items for each pixel. It is for this reason that the loop counter is set to add 4 for each iteration:

```
for (var i = 0; i < pixelData.data.length; i += 4 ) {
    ...
}
```

For each pixel, you then need to extract the relevant red, green, and blue information for that pixel. The alpha channel data is not required in this example, so you can safely ignore it:

```
var r = pixelData.data[i]; // red channel
var g = pixelData.data[i + 1]; // green channel
var b = pixelData.data[i + 2]; // blue channel
```

Now that you have this information, you need to convert it to grey. A number of methods are available to do this, the simplest of which is to calculate the average colour across all three values:

```
var averageColour = (r + g + b) / 3;
```

You then set each red, green, and blue value for each of the pixels to be this new average colour:

```
pixelData.data[i] = averageColour;
pixelData.data[i + 1] = averageColour;
pixelData.data[i + 2] = averageColour;
```

Finally, you need to write the newly manipulated image and its data to the actual display canvas context:

```
context.putImageData(pixelData, 0, 0);
```

TIP: If you're creating this example as you follow along, it won't work unless you run it through a web server. A local file will be considered "cross-origin" (i.e., from another website), so the API will forbid you from obtaining an image from it and manipulating its pixels. This cross-origin security policy exists to prevent files on one domain from accessing and altering information from a file on another domain without permission.

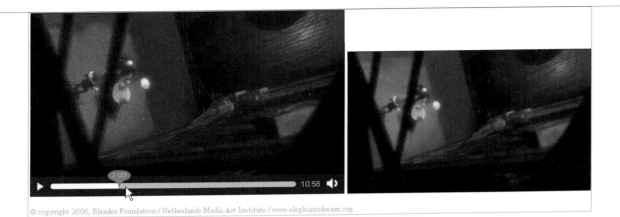

FIGURE 9.5 A greyscale copy of the original video is displayed in the canvas element on the right.

Of course, right now this code doesn't do anything: You need to ensure that the `makeItGrey()` function actually gets called.

Mimicking what you did in the second example, the function can simply be set up to be called at 33-millisecond intervals using the `setInterval()` function when the video is set to play:

```
video.addEventListener('play', function() {
    setInterval("makeItGrey()", 33);
}, false);
```

And presto, the video copy is displayed on the canvas but this time in greyscale (**Figure 9.5**).

There's a lot more that you can do with canvas and with pixel manipulation. This chapter provided just a small insight into what you can achieve. If what you've read has piqued your interest, plenty of good online tutorials (e.g., www.html5rocks.com/en/tutorials/#canvas) and books are available that you can follow up with, and I encourage you to do so. Go and play!

WRAPPING **UP**

The canvas element and the 2D JavaScript API have a lot of potential, and indeed, many games and JavaScript libraries are beginning to use them to their full potential.

Because you can draw a video directly onto a canvas, it allows you to do simple tasks like take screen shots and keep a copy of a playing video in sync with a version in the canvas. You can also manipulate pixels by obtaining the image data and then drawing it back onto the canvas.

The next chapter also focuses on video and images, but this time with another format that has been in existence before HTML5 but seems to have come to the forefront since HTML5 has become more popular. Scalable Vector Graphics (SVG) is up next.

10

USING **VIDEO** WITH **SVG**

Scalable Vector Graphics (SVG) is a language that allows you to define two-dimensional vector graphics for display in your web documents. Written in XML and supported by all of the major browsers, you can use it to describe vector shapes, text, and images on which you can also apply specific filters.

SVG has been around for a while but seems to have escaped the notice of most web developers. This has changed with the advent of HTML5 and the `svg` element and the fact that it is now supported by Internet Explorer 9. As people became more interested in canvas (which you read about in Chapter 9) and its capabilities, they also began to take more notice of SVG and what it might be capable of.

This chapter briefly explores SVG and how you can use it to achieve a number of effects with HTML5 media elements, more specifically the `video` element.

A BRIEF **INTRODUCTION** TO **SVG**

The SVG specification is not part of HTML5 but has been in development with the W3C since 1999 as an open standard. Version 1.1 is the current recommendation since 2001. A new version, 1.2, is a recent working draft, but it is version 1.1 that this chapter will mainly discuss.

As mentioned in the chapter introduction, SVG is written in XML, and the browser uses this XML definition to render the required shape, text, or image. In effect, the XML file will contain drawing instructions for the browser to interpret and use to render the required graphics—for example, coordinates of points to draw lines to, text to include, and different curves and shapes. This of course means that the only data that needs to be downloaded by the browser for it to display the graphic(s) in question is an XML text file rather than potentially larger image files.

Another advantage of SVG is that the graphics produced are vector graphics rather than raster graphics, so the image will be scaled cleanly by the browser within the available space should it need to be.

RASTER AND **VECTOR GRAPHICS**

FIGURE 10.1 The difference in quality between raster (top) and vector graphics (bottom) when scaled up.

A raster graphics image, or bitmap, is a data structure that contains pixel information for a graphic. Because the graphic defined by this pixel information depends on all the pixel information available, it is dependent on the resolution the original image was created in. For this reason, it doesn't scale up very well because it doesn't have enough pixel information for the new size, which leads to a loss of quality. Raster graphics also lead to large file sizes because they contain information on each pixel in the image.

Vector graphics, on the other hand, are defined via geometrical information, such as points, curves, lines, shapes, and so on, all of which are based on mathematical equations. The tool drawing the image, in this case a web browser, uses this geometrical information to redraw the graphic, allowing it to build the best-quality image possible given the screen resolution. Vector graphic files are smaller in size than raster graphic files because they only contain formulas to create the required shapes rather than individual pixel information.

Figure 10.1 illustrates the difference between raster and vector graphics when an image is scaled up.

You can also apply features such as filter effects and clipping paths to SVG graphics, and animate them as well. You'll see examples of some of these added features later in the chapter.

The SVG specification is quite large, and a rundown of all its capabilities is outside the scope of this chapter. You can view the latest specification, version 1.1, at the W3C at www.w3.org/TR/SVG11. Only those features and elements that are used in the examples in this chapter will be described here.

Let's look at how well-supported SVG is amongst the main browsers.

BROWSER SUPPORT

Because it's been around for so long, and with Internet Explorer finally joining in with version 9, SVG is now supported by the latest versions of the major browsers. However, as mentioned earlier, the SVG specification is huge, so different parts of it are supported by different browsers.

An amazingly in-depth table of how well SVG is supported across the major browsers is maintained by Jeff Schiller, co-chair of the W3C SVG Interest Group at www.codedread.com/svg-support-table.html (you can see a condensed version at www.codedread.com/svg-support.php). Overall, the main features are supported by Firefox, Safari, Chrome, Opera, and Internet Explorer 9 and later.

There is a caveat to this support with regards to HTML5 media. The "main features" of SVG that are widely supported relate to those you would use when drawing images and text within a web document. Support is not as widespread with regards to filters or masking, or anything that this chapter will show you with regards to SVG interactions with HTML5 videos. Currently, only Firefox and Safari support the SVG features that you will see in this chapter.

XML SVG definitions are usually contained within an external XML file with a .svg extension, which is then embedded in a web document via such elements as embed and object. HTML5 changes the requirement for an external file with the introduction of the svg element, which allows you to define SVG definitions within an HTML5 web document.

THE SVG ELEMENT

The svg element is part of the HTML5 specification and allows you to define SVG shapes, text, and graphics within a web document without having to embed an external SVG file.

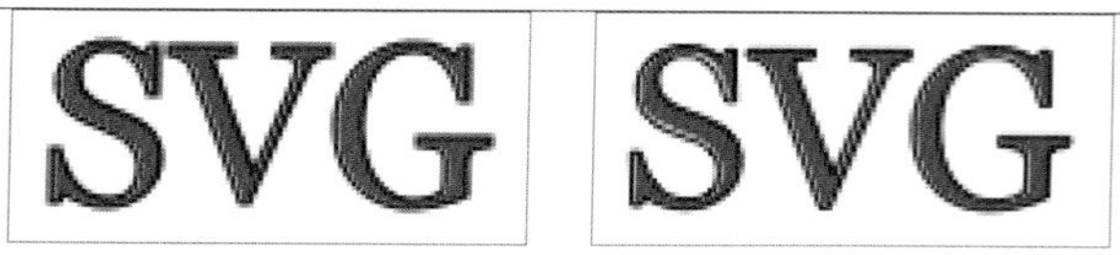

FIGURE 10.2 Simple text rendering in SVG in Firefox 5 (left) and Safari 5.1 (right).

You can also use the svg element to define SVG code that will be used elsewhere in the document for functions such as masking and animation. You will see it used in this way later in some examples in this chapter.

The latest versions of all the major browsers currently support the svg element, except for Opera, which will support it in version 12. You can view an updated browser support table for the svg element at http://caniuse.com/svg-html5.

Let's take a quick look at some of the simplest SVG elements that are available for you to use.

NOTES: If you want an SVG definition to display in Opera 11.50, you can embed it as an external SVG file and it will work fine, as it will in all the other major browsers.

You can read more about the svg element at http://dev.w3.org/html5/spec/Overview.html#svg-0.

SVG TEXT

The SVG text element allows you to specify a graphics element that consists of text. It can take a number of attributes—a full list of which is available at www.w3.org/TR/SVG11/text.html#TextElement. But here you will only use a few of the attributes.

In this example, let's display the letters SVG using an SVG text element. The SVG code required for this is as follows:

```
<svg>
    <text x="0" y="50" font-size="50" font-family="Georgia"
    → fill="#cd0000" stroke="black" stroke-width="1">SVG</text>
</svg>
```

This code defines the position of the text using X and Y values, and also uses the fill attribute to set the text colour to a reddish colour. The size and family of the font is set using the font-size and font-family attributes, respectively. A black outline of width 1 is also added to the text via the stroke and stroke-width attributes.

Figure 10.2 shows how the resulting text is rendered in Firefox and Safari.

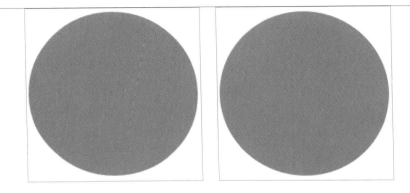

FIGURE 10.3 A circle drawn in SVG in Chrome 13 (left) and Firefox 5 (right).

SVG CIRCLE

One of the simplest shapes that you might want to draw via SVG is a circle. This is relatively easy because SVG provides the circle element for your convenience:

```
<svg height="200">
    <circle cx="100" cy="100" r="100" fill="#0e8c3a" />
</svg>
```

This code defines the position of the circle using X and Y coordinates but this time using the cx and cy attributes. The radius of the circle is set to 100 using the r attribute. Once again fill is used to specify the colour of the circle, in this case a type of green.

Figure 10.3 shows you how the circle looks in a browser.

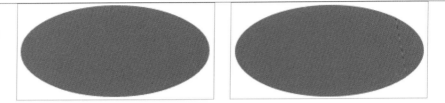

FIGURE 10.4 A bluish ellipse in Safari 5.1 (left) and Chrome 13 (right).

SVG ELLIPSE

You can also draw an ellipse, which is a circle elongated in one direction. To draw an ellipse, as well as the X and Y positions of the shape, you also need to specify the radius width and height:

```
<svg height="200">
    <ellipse cx="100" cy="100" rx="100" ry="50" fill="#0276fd" />
</svg>
```

The `fill` colour here is set to a shade of blue, and the width and height of the radius is now defined using the `rx` and `ry` attributes respectively.

Note: You could of course use the `ellipse` element to draw a circle if you set the `rx` and `ry` attributes to the same value, but obviously it's best to use the `circle` element because that's what it's there for!

You can see how this simple ellipse renders in **Figure 10.4**.

The previous examples show only a very small taste of how you can draw shapes and text using SVG. There's a whole lot more that you can do with SVG, so I encourage you to seek out more information and play around with it.

TIP: For some online SVG resources, go to http://www.learnsvg.com and http://my.opera.com/tagawa/blog/learning-svg.

Next, you'll use this basic SVG knowledge to interact with the HTML5 `video` element.

USING **SVG** WITH **HTML5 VIDEO**

In the previous section you were introduced to some of the simpler features of drawing SVG text and shapes. In this section, you'll learn how to use those simple text and shape definitions in conjunction with the HTML5 video element as masks, and you'll also apply some nifty filters to your video that SVG provides as well.

> **NOTE:** All the examples listed in this chapter are available on the book's companion website at www.html5multimedia.com.

ADDING A TEXT MASK TO A VIDEO

In Chapter 6, you learned how to add a mask over a video in WebKit browsers using the –webkit-mask-box-image CSS property. Well, you can also add masks over video via SVG. You just define an SVG graphic as the mask and use it on your video.

Note: Using inline SVG (i.e., with the SVG definition within the web document via the svg element) to mask elements currently only works in Firefox.

For this first example, you'll add a text mask over the video. The video being played will only be visible where the text exists.

For these examples, let's again use the colourful parrots video:

```
<video autoplay controls>
    <source src="parrots-small.mp4" type="video/mp4">
    <source src="parrots-small.webm" type="video/webm">
</video>
```

To define a mask in SVG, you simply enclose it within the mask element. Also, give the mask element a unique identifier of "vmask", because you'll need to reference it later:

```
<svg>
    <mask id="vmask">
        <text x="10" y="140" font-size="200" font-family="Verdana"
        → font-weight="bold" fill="#fff">H5</text>
    </mask>
</svg>
```

FIGURE 10.5 The H5 text mask over the parrot video in Firefox 5.

In the preceding code example, within the mask element, a text element is defined using the text "H5" with various attributes, the most noteworthy of which is the fill attribute. When you're defining a mask, you must use white as the fill colour for the element the mask is being applied to so that it will be fully visible through the mask.

TIP: One great advantage of SVG is that the elements that you define within it are available through the DOM (Document Object Model) for referencing and use later in SVG and by JavaScript or CSS.

For the code to actually do anything, you then need to apply the mask to the video element, which you do via the mask property in the CSS definition for the video element:

```
video {
    mask:url('#vmask');
}
```

The value the mask property is set to is the unique identifier you assigned to the mask element earlier, in this case "vmask".

You can see how this renders in Firefox 5 in **Figure 10.5**.

Unfortunately, this example only works in Firefox because it uses inline SVG to define the mask. But you can get it to work in Safari if you place the mask definition in an external SVG file and reference that.

The external file text.svg is thus defined as follows:

```
<?xml version="1.0" standalone="no"?>
<!DOCTYPE svg PUBLIC "-//W3C//DTD SVG 1.1//EN"
→ "http://www.w3.org/Graphics/SVG/1.1/DTD/svg11.dtd">
<svg version="1.1" xmlns="http://www.w3.org/2000/svg"
→ xmlns:xlink="http://www.w3.org/1999/xlink">
    <defs>
        <mask>
            <text id="text" x="10" y="140" font-size="200"
            → font-weight="bold" font-family="Verdana"
            → fill="white">H5</text>
        </mask>
    </defs>
    <use xlink:href="#text" />
</svg>
```

Because this SVG file is an XML file, you place the XML header at the top:

```
<?xml version="1.0" standalone="no"?>
```

The standalone attribute is set to no, indicating that the XML document does not stand alone and depends on an externally defined DTD.

WHAT'S A DTD?

A Document Type Definition (DTD) is a set of markup declarations that defines the structure of a markup document. The DTD defines the legal elements and attributes that the markup document can contain.

The next line is the SVG doctype declaration, which indicates that the document content follows the SVG 1.1 DTD:

```
<!DOCTYPE svg PUBLIC "-//W3C//DTD SVG 1.1//EN"
 → "http://www.w3.org/Graphics/SVG/1.1/DTD/svg11.dtd">
```

The svg element then appears, indicating the version and XML namespace (in this case, SVG) and including a reference to the xlink document definition, which is required a bit farther down in the XML file (where it'll be explained):

```
<svg version="1.1" xmlns="http://www.w3.org/2000/svg"
 → xmlns:xlink="http://www.w3.org/1999/xlink">
```

The defs element is used to contain any SVG definitions that will not immediately be rendered onscreen but can be used later.

The mask and text element definitions contain the same code as the same inline SVG definitions in the earlier example; the only exception is that the text element is given the unique identifier "text". This identifier is used in the next line in the file:

```
<use xlink:href="#text" />
```

This line, which makes use of the xlink document definition linked to earlier, informs the document that on loading to use the resource pointed to in the xlink:href attribute, in this case the text element definition.

TIP: Using the use element with xlink:href also allows you to reuse code within the SVG file without having to duplicate it.

You then need to reference the external text.svg file from the original HTML5 file. In the CSS definition for the video, you used the WebKit-specific property -webkit-mask to point to the SVG file:

```
video {
    mask:url('#vmask');
    -webkit-mask:url('text.svg');
}
```

FIGURE 10.6 The H5 text mask as rendered in Safari 5.1.

FIGURE 10.7 The rather broken implementation of text masking in Chrome 13.

And presto, the text mask now also works in Safari 5.1 (**Figure 10.6**)!

Because Chrome is also a WebKit browser, you're probably wondering if this text mask works with Chrome. Unfortunately, it doesn't work properly; the text is simply written over the video (**Figure 10.7**). Hopefully, this will be fixed in a future version of the browser.

Now that you've learned how to apply a text mask to an HTML5 video, you can use the same principles to apply another SVG mask, this time using a shape.

NOTE: In the supplied examples, you might notice that the video controls are still available to be clicked beneath the SVG mask (if you can guess where they're located!). This could be quite useful because you can apply the mask without necessarily having to implement your own custom control set.

ADDING AN ELLIPSE MASK TO A VIDEO

Earlier in this chapter, you learned that you can use SVG to define and draw an ellipse. Just like the text element, you can also use the ellipse element to define a mask that you can place over your HTML5 video.

The principles are of course the same as in the preceding text mask example. In this example, you'll define the ellipse mask in an external SVG file. It's worth learning how to reference such a file for Firefox as well as for Safari.

The video you'll use in this example is the same as the preceding example:

```
<video autoplay controls>
    <source src="parrots-small.mp4" type="video/mp4">
    <source src="parrots-small.webm" type="video/webm">
</video>
```

You define the SVG mask in the external SVG XML file ellipse.svg—the definition of which is very similar to the text mask example—but you replace the text element with an ellipse element definition:

```
<?xml version="1.0" standalone="no"?>
<!DOCTYPE svg PUBLIC "-//W3C//DTD SVG 1.1//EN"
 → "http://www.w3.org/Graphics/SVG/1.1/DTD/svg11.dtd">

<svg version="1.1" xmlns="http://www.w3.org/2000/svg"
 → xmlns:xlink="http://www.w3.org/1999/xlink">
    <defs>
        <mask id="eMask">
            <ellipse id="ellipse" cx="150" cy="80" rx="150" ry="80"
             → fill="white" />
        </mask>
    </defs>
    <use xlink:href="#ellipse"/>
</svg>
```

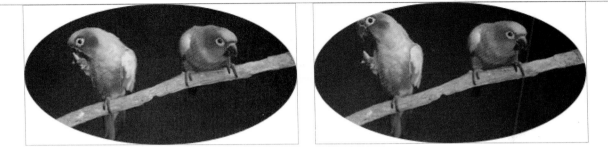

FIGURE 10.8 The ellipse mask rendered in Firefox (left) and Safari (right).

The mask element has a unique identifier of "eMask" because you'll need it for referencing. The ellipse has a unique identifier of "ellipse" and is defined with X and Y coordinates, a radius of 150 on the X axis, and a radius of 80 on the Y axis. The fill colour is white, as is required for masks.

The use element links to the ellipse element contained within the mask element.

In the calling HTML file, the CSS declaration uses the -webkit-mask-box-image property to target WebKit browsers. For Firefox, you use the mask property, and make sure its url value also references the mask's identifier, "eMask", as well as the SVG file:

```
video {
    mask:url('ellipse.svg#eMask');
    -webkit-mask-box-image:url('ellipse.svg');
}
```

And that's it. You can see how this renders in Firefox and Safari in **Figure 10.8**.

As you can imagine, you could define any shape in SVG and then use it as a mask for an HTML5 video should you want to show only some of the video to achieve the desired effect.

Once you've defined your mask, you may also want to animate it for an added effect.

NOTE: For browsers that don't support SVG masks, the video will simply be displayed normally.

ANIMATING AN SVG VIDEO MASK

SVG also allows you to define animations on the graphics that you've defined, and because masks are simply graphics, you can apply animations to them as well.

NOTE: The animation examples could also use inline SVG to define the SVG masks but would only work for Firefox. Therefore, all SVG definitions are declared in external files so they work in Firefox and Safari.

The same video declaration used in the two preceding examples is again utilised for this example, so the code won't be repeated here.

The main areas of interest are the SVG file, which is called `animate-ellipse.svg` here, and how the animation is defined:

```
<?xml version="1.0" standalone="no"?>
<!DOCTYPE svg PUBLIC "-//W3C//DTD SVG 1.1//EN"
→  "http://www.w3.org/Graphics/SVG/1.1/DTD/svg11.dtd">

<svg version="1.1" xmlns="http://www.w3.org/2000/svg"
→  xmlns:xlink="http://www.w3.org/1999/xlink">
    <defs>
        <mask id="eMask">
            <ellipse id="ellipse" cx="150" cy="80" rx="100" ry="80"
            →  fill="white">
                <animate attributeName="rx" dur="3s"
                →  values="100;150;100" repeatCount="5" />
            </ellipse>
        </mask>
    </defs>
    <use xlink:href="#ellipse"/>
</svg>
```

Once again, everything is declared within a `mask` element, and the `ellipse` element declaration is largely the same as the preceding example except that the radius along the X axis is now defined as 100.

There is also an animate element, which, of course, defines the animation used:

```
<animate attributeName="rx" dur="3s" values="100;150;100"
    repeatCount="5" />
```

The animation in this case simply changes the ellipse's radius from 100 to 150 and back again. The animate element is used to animate a single attribute or property over a given duration of time.

The attributeName attribute identifies the ellipse's attribute that will be animated, in this case the X radius, so it's set to rx. The dur attribute indicates how long the animation will take, the duration, which is set to 3s (3 seconds). The values attribute is a semicolon-separated list of the values the animation will animate from and to, from 100 to 150 and back to 100 again. And repeatCount refers to how many times the animation will be repeated, in this case 5.

> **NOTE:** You can read more about the animate element at www.w3.org/TR/SVG11/animate.html#AnimateElement.

With the SVG file defined, the only thing left to do is assign it to the video using the CSS properties you've already used, namely mask and -webkit-mask-box-image:

```
video {
    mask:url('animate-ellipse.svg#eMask');
    -webkit-mask-box-image:url('animate-ellipse.svg');
}
```

Figure 10.9 gives you a rough idea of how this animation might work in practice.

Let's take this animation one step further and look at how you can actually create an animation that animates the mask from one position to another rather than animating a static shape.

FIGURE 10.9 The X radius of the ellipse mask animates from 100 (A) to 150 (C) through the animation transition state represented by image B.

MOVING AN SVG VIDEO MASK

The preceding example showed you how the attributes of an SVG mask can be animated. You can also animate the entire mask, moving it along a predefined path, which is what you'll do in this example.

You'll use the same video code in this example, and once again it will only work in Firefox and Safari.

The mask in this example is a small circle, and the animation will move the circle mask from the first parrot's head across to the other parrot's head in a linear motion, showing each one in turn.

So, once again, the SVG file, circle-animate-motion.svg, is where the action happens:

```
<?xml version="1.0" standalone="no"?>
<!DOCTYPE svg PUBLIC "-//W3C//DTD SVG 1.1//EN"
  "http://www.w3.org/Graphics/SVG/1.1/DTD/svg11.dtd">

<svg version="1.1" xmlns="http://www.w3.org/2000/svg"
  xmlns:xlink="http://www.w3.org/1999/xlink">
    <defs>
        <mask id="cMask">
            <path id="path" d="M 0 0 L 130 0" />
            <circle id="circle" cx="85" cy="30" r="40" fill="white">
                <animateMotion begin="0s" dur="2s" fill="freeze">
                    <mpath xlink:href="#path" />
                </animateMotion>
            </circle>
        </mask>
    </defs>
    <use xlink:href="#circle"/>
</svg>
```

As usual, everything is contained within a mask element, which has an identifier of "cMask".

The next line is something new, a path element definition.

```
<path id="path" d="M 0 0 L 130 0" />
```

You use the path element to define a predetermined path for animation. This particular one has an identifier of "path" and the d attribute contains the actual path data. The path data can contain a number of definitions for the path's route, beginning with a "moveto" command, which uses M to establish a new point for the animation, much like lifting a pen from a page and placing it elsewhere. In this example, the "moveto" point is set to the X and Y coordinates 0,0.

Next, you use the "lineto" command, which you indicate with an L, to define X and Y coordinates that draw a line to and from the current point. In this example, the "lineto" command is 130,0, so the path is in effect specifying: "draw a line from point 0,0 to point 130,0".

NOTE: The animation example uses the simplest path definition possible. You can define other, more complicated paths that follow Bezier curves and the like. You can read more about path data at www.w3.org/TR/SVG11/paths.html#PathData.

The circle has an initial position of 85 on the X axis and 30 on the Y, and it has a radius of 40. Again, the fill colour is set to white.

The circle element also contains the definition for the animate motion via the animateMotion element:

```
<animateMotion begin="1s" dur="4s" fill="freeze">

    <mpath xlink:href="#path" />

</animateMotion>
```

The animateMotion element here has a number of attributes. The begin attribute specifies when the animation will begin; here it is set to 1s, so there's a delay of 1 second before the animation starts. The dur attribute indicates how long the animation will take, in this case 4 seconds.

The fill attribute is set to freeze, which tells the animation to stay in the position it ended up at when the animation is complete.

NOTE: You can read more about the animateMotion element at www.w3.org/TR/SVG11/animate.html#AnimateMotionElement.

FIGURE 10.10 The animation as it appears in Safari. The circle mask moves across the video from one parrot (A) to the other (C) via an animation state (B).

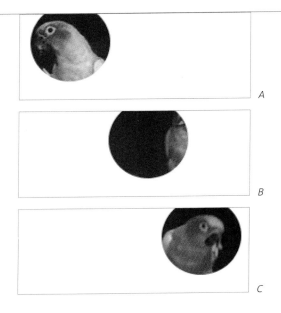

A

B

C

The mpath element informs the browser that the path that the animation will follow is the predefined path with the "path" identifier, which is the path you defined earlier.

All that's left to do now is to assign the SVG to the video:

```
video {
    mask:url('circle-animate-motion.svg#cMask');
    -webkit-mask:url('circle-animate-motion.svg');
}
```

Figure 10.10 shows how this might look when viewed in either Firefox or Safari.

There's a lot that you can do with SVG masks, and the previous examples show only a small bit of what is possible. Using the preceding examples as a starting point, be sure to experiment with SVG masks and try to enhance your web videos.

Before you stop thinking about SVG and HTML5 video, let's look at another exciting capability of SVG and HTML5 video—filters.

APPLYING SVG FILTERS TO HTML5 VIDEO

SVG has a large number of filters that you can apply to SVG graphic elements. Although the W3C specification doesn't specify it, Mozilla has taken it one step further and allows you to apply SVG filters to HTML5 media elements as well, specifically the video element. This can lead to some very cool effects but needs to be used with caution because SVG filters currently only work on HTML5 media elements in Firefox. This might change in the future, but there is no guarantee that it will.

Because Firefox alone supports these features on HTML5 media elements, the examples in this section use inline SVG and target only that browser.

NOTE: The filters mentioned in this section can of course be applied to any SVG graphic elements.

Let's briefly look at two of the filters, feColorMatrix and feGaussianBlur. You can view the full list, and indeed learn more about the filter element, at www.w3.org/TR/SVG11/filters.html#FilterElement.

THE FECOLORMATRIX FILTER

The feColorMatrix filter allows you to apply a matrix transformation to the SVG graphics object in question. These matrices can be quite complex and a bit beyond me to be honest, but there are a number of predefined settings that you can apply via the type attribute. The following four examples walk you through each setting in turn, showing you how it is applied and what its effect is.

Each filter element definition is contained within a defs element within an svg element, a layout you should by now be familiar with:

```
<svg>
    <defs>
        <filter......>
            ......
        </filter>
    </defs>
</svg>
```

The following examples contain the filter element definition only.

FIGURE 10.11 A saturation filter with a value of 0.2 is applied to the video.

FIGURE 10.12 The pixel hue of the video is rotated by an angle of 50 degrees.

COLOUR SATURATION

Applying the colour saturation matrix filter allows you to saturate the colours of your video. You can supply one value to the values attribute, which is a single real number between 0 and 1 that allows you to adjust the saturation of the colour:

```
<filter id="saturate">
    <feColorMatrix type="saturate" values="0.2" />
</filter>
```

This code applies a saturation of 0.2, the result of which can you can see in **Figure 10.11**.

HUE ROTATION

A video will use a certain amount of colours in a colour spectrum. This colour spectrum is arranged in a circle, and it is possible to move from one part of the colour spectrum to another by performing a hue rotation by rotating a number of degrees around the circular colour spectrum.

The hueRotate type allows you to perform a hue rotation on the video by an angle specified by the values attribute, which must be a valid degree value:

```
<filter id="hueRotate">
    <feColorMatrix type="hueRotate" values="50" />
</filter>
```

This code applies the hueRotate type with a rotation angle of 50 degrees. You can see the result in **Figure 10.12**.

FIGURE 10.13 The video with the `luminanceToAlpha` colour matrix type applied to it (left). The large white areas are transparent, and a background image would show through them, as shown on the right, where you can barely make out the parrots and the branch.

LUMINANCE TO ALPHA

Applying the `luminanceToAlpha` colour matrix type converts the red, green, and blue (RGB) channels of the video pixels into a luminance value and then sets the output alpha channel of each pixel based on the result (**Figure 10.13**). This in effect sets the transparency values of individual pixels based on the luminance, or relative brightness, of the pixels. There are no attributes for this type:

```
<filter id="luminanceToAlpha">

    <feColorMatrix type="luminanceToAlpha" />

</filter>
```

BLACK AND WHITE

To convert the video to black and white, you need to supply the actual matrix values to the `filter` element via the `values` attribute:

```
<filter id="blackAndWhiteMatrix">

    <feColorMatrix type="matrix" values="0.3 0.3 0.3 0 0

                                         0.3 0.3 0.3 0 0

                                         0.3 0.3 0.3 0 0

                                         0   0   0   1 0" />

</filter>
```

The result of applying these matrix values is shown in **Figure 10.14** on the next page.

FIGURE 10.14 A matrix is applied to the video that converts the pixels to their black-and-white versions.

FIGURE 10.15 A Gaussian blur is applied to the video. The controls would also be blurred, so you need to remove them and create your own, as explained in Chapter 5.

Using the `matrix` type, as shown in the preceding black-and-white example, allows you to apply your own matrix transform to the video pixels. To use it effectively, you'll need to have an understanding of matrix multiplication, which has long since vacated my brain I'm afraid.

NOTE: You can read more about the `feColorMatrix` filter at www.w3.org/TR/SVG11/filters.html#feColorMatrixElement.

Let's move on to take a quick look at another filter, `feGaussianBlur`.

THE FEGAUSSIANBLUR FILTER

The `feGaussianBlur` filter allows you to add a blur to the video. It takes one attribute, `stdDeviation`, which can contain either one or two numbers. If two numbers are provided, the first one indicates the standard deviation along the X axis, and the second number provides the standard deviation value along the Y axis. A single number provides the same value for both the X and Y axes:

```
<filter id="blur">
    <feGaussianBlur stdDeviation="2" />
</filter>
```

This code applies a Gaussian blur with a standard deviation value of 2. The result is shown in **Figure 10.15**.

You can also merge filters and apply more than one to the same element, which, of course, you are encouraged to experiment with. Again, bear in mind that only Firefox allows these filters to be applied to the HTML5 video element, so they should be treated as experimental while this remains so.

You can use HTML5 video within SVG content as well, for example, within an external SVG file. But that's strictly SVG content related, not HTML, so is considered outside the scope of this book.

WRAPPING UP

You've now had a basic introduction to SVG. SVG has been around for a long time, and fortunately people are beginning to wake up to the fact that it can be beneficial to the quick loading of their websites, and of course, the smooth rendering of simple graphics.

You learned how you can use SVG to interact with your HTML5 video as masks or filters. You also need to remember that not all browsers fully support this interaction and therefore you should use SVG with caution.

In the next chapter, you'll look at the future of HTML5 in relation to multimedia and what other functionality and APIs will possibly be available for use soon.

11

FUTURE **FEATURES**

Although this is the final chapter in the book, it is by no means the final chapter with regards to HTML5 and multimedia. You've learned about many HTML5 audio and video features, but other specifications are currently being developed that contain some new related functionality that will be of great benefit once they are finished and browser vendors begin to implement them.

This chapter briefly discusses some of these specifications and their content. Although they are not strictly part of HTML5, they do contain functionality that will enhance existing HTML5 features. These features are JavaScript APIs that will enable you to create and manipulate audio, interact with external devices, such as webcams and microphones, and facilitate video conferencing. Although most of these features are not yet implemented in browsers, it's worthwhile learning about where they are headed.

AUDIO **APIs**

As you've read through this book, you've probably been aware that more was said about video than about audio. This section works toward restoring that balance by exploring APIs that affect audio only (although the information also applies to video, of course, because audio exists in most video!).

At the moment, two proposed JavaScript APIs are available that allow you to read and write raw audio data. One is the Web Audio API, which was created by Google and is currently under discussion by the W3C Audio Working Group. This Working Group was created in March 2011, and its chartered mission is to:

> "develop a client-side script API adding more advanced audio capabilities than are currently offered by audio elements. The API will support the features required by advanced interactive applications including the ability to process and synthesize audio streams directly in script, and will extend the HTML5 <audio> and <video> media elements."

Mozilla has also created an audio API, which is simpler than the Web Audio API and has shipped it with Firefox 4 and later (https://wiki.mozilla.org/Audio_Data_API). Mozilla's Audio Data API is an extension to the HTML5 Media API that you read about in Chapter 5.

As you can probably guess, because these APIs have been created by different browser vendors, the parts of their respective APIs that do currently work only do so in their respective browsers. However, this isn't as much of an issue right now, because they are only proposed APIs, and nothing has been decided yet.

Let's look at the Audio Data API by Mozilla first.

AUDIO DATA API

Mozilla's Audio Data API provides an extension to programmatically access and/or create raw audio data in HTML5 audio and video files.

READING AUDIO DATA

As audio is being played (either via an audio or video element) and decoded, sample data is stored in a framebuffer. When this framebuffer has data available for use, the MozAudioAvailable event is raised. The sample data contained within the framebuffer is raw audio data, which may or may not have been played at the time the MozAudioAvailable event is raised.

Recall the loadedmetadata event mentioned in Chapter 5, which is raised when an audio or video element has useful metadata loaded. When waiting to read audio data, you can use this event as well. Once it is raised, the Audio Data API then has three new attributes that can be accessed that contain vital information for raw audio data:

- mozChannels. Indicates the number of audio channels.

- mozSampleRate. Specifies the audio sample rate per second.

- mozFrameBufferLength. Indicates the default size of the framebuffer.

Let's look at an example that displays the data provided by these three attributes. You first define the audio element and a simple div to contain the audio information:

```
<audio id="audio" controls>
    <source src="piano.ogg" type="audio/ogg">
</audio>
<div id="info"></div>
```

NOTE: A Vorbis/Ogg audio file is used in this example because the Audio Data API works only in Firefox.

When the audio data is loaded, you access the data using the API:

```
var audio = document.getElementById("audio");
var info = document.getElementById("info");
audio.addEventListener("loadedmetadata", getAudioData, false);
function getAudioData() {
    var rate = audio.mozSampleRate;
    var channels = audio.mozChannels;
    var length = audio.mozFrameBufferLength;
    info.innerHTML = "rate: " + rate + "<br/>channels: " + channels
+ "</br>length: " + length;
}
```

FIGURE 11.1 The audio file's sample rate, channels, and buffer length are displayed onscreen in Firefox 6.

rate: 44100
channels: 2
length: 2048

In this code sample, handles to the audio and div element are obtained. When the loadedmetadata event is raised, the data in the three attributes—mozSampleRate, mozChannels, and mozFrameBufferLength—is read, and their data is displayed onscreen in the div (**Figure 11.1**).

You can access the framebuffer data through the MozAudioAvailable event's frameBuffer attribute, which is an array of decoded audio sample data in float number format.

Let's extend the preceding example by adding another div for displaying the framebuffer data and then defining a new function, getBufferData, that you attach to the MozAudioAvailable event. The getBufferData function simply outputs the first element of the databuffer array to the screen:

```
<audio id="audio" controls>
    <source src="piano.ogg" type="audio/ogg">
</audio>
<div id="info"></div>
<div id="frameinfo"></div>
```

And the JavaScript code (only showing the new additions) looks like this:

```
var frameinfo = document.getElementById("frameinfo");
audio.addEventListener("MozAudioAvailable", getBufferData, false);
function getBufferData(event) {
    frameinfo.innerHTML += "[" + event.frameBuffer[0] + "]";
}
```

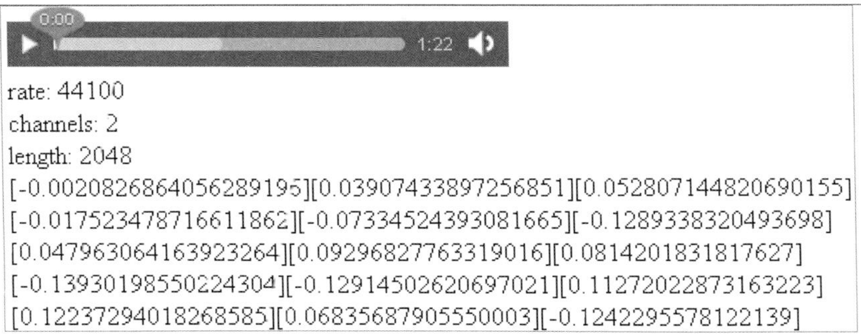

```
 0:00
 ▶ |⚫————————————    1:22 ◀)
rate: 44100
channels: 2
length: 2048
[-0.0020826864056289195][0.03907433897256851][0.052807144820690155]
[-0.017523478716611862][-0.07334524393081665][-0.1289338320493698]
[0.047963064163923264][0.09296827763319016][0.0814201831817627]
[-0.13930198550224304][-0.12914502620697021][0.11272022873163223]
[0.12237294018268585][0.06835687905550003][-0.1242295578122139]
```

FIGURE 11.2 The audio file's framebuffer data shown onscreen as the audio is being played.

The data that is displayed onscreen is the float values of the audio data, as shown in **Figure 11.2**.

This may not look very useful right now, but you can use this data to visualise the audio as it's playing in a waveform or fast Fourier transform.

You can also use the Audio Data API to write to an audio element.

> **NOTE:** An example of an audio file's data being displayed as a waveform is on the www.html5multimedia.com website.

WRITING AUDIO DATA

The Audio Data API provides three methods that allow you to create your own audio:

- `mozSetup(channels,sampleRate)`. Sets up an audio element with a specified number of channels and sample rate.

- `mozWriteAudio(buffer)`. Writes audio buffer data (an array) to an audio element.

- `mozCurrentSampleOffset()`. Returns the current position of the current audio stream.

You can call these methods on an audio element, which can be an existing HTML element to which you have obtained a handle (as you did in the preceding examples), or you can create one dynamically using the Audio() constructor.

The following example generates and plays a simple tone when the user clicks a Play button:

```
<button onclick="play()">play</button>
```

The play function is then declared as:

```
function play() {
    var audioOut = new Audio();
    audioOut.mozSetup(2, 44100);
    var audioSamples = new Float32Array(88200);
    for (var i=0; i<audioSamples.length; i++) {
        audioSamples[i] = Math.sin(i/60);
    }
    audioOut.mozWriteAudio(audioSamples);
}
```

This code example creates a new audio element and then sets it up to have two audio channels at a sample rate of 44100. A float array is then defined with twice the number of samples, and this array is then populated with simple sine-wave data (the divisor of 60 was chosen at random).

When a user clicks the Play button, a single long tone is produced. There's no point in trying to show you this in an image, so you'll have to either try the example in Firefox or go to www.html5multimedia.com and listen to it!

Although very simple, this example shows you how you can generate audio data with the API. You could also read in the data from one audio element, manipulate it (perhaps you might want to change the pitch or tone), and then write it out to another audio element. This, and more, is all possible through this simple Audio Data API.

NOTE: For additional resources and more in-depth demonstrations of the Audio Data API, go to https://wiki.mozilla.org/Audio_Data_API#Additional_Resources.

Let's now look at the more complex Web Audio API that's currently under consideration by the W3C.

WEB AUDIO API

The draft specification for the Web Audio API is rather large and complex, with a whole range of different interfaces and methods defined to give you a tremendous amount of control over your audio.

This section just gives you a brief introduction to the API, so you won't read about everything that the API has to offer. But you can read the specification at https://dvcs.w3.org/hg/audio/raw-file/tip/webaudio/specification.html.

The goal of the Web Audio API is to support the following features:

- Processing of media sources from audio and video elements

- Modular routing for simple or complex effect architectures

- Audio stream synthesis and processing

- Spatialised audio for 3D games and immersive environments (e.g., distance attenuation, sound cones, and Doppler shift)

- A convolution engine to support a wide range of linear sound playback effects, such as cathedral, concert hall, cave, and amphitheatre

This list of features is not exhaustive; you can read about more supported features in the specification. Don't worry if some of the items in the list don't mean anything to you. They don't mean much to me either because I'm not a sound engineer and have never worked with complex audio. Others should be familiar to you, and you can see how the ability to create different spatialised audio, for example, would be beneficial for game development.

It's quite difficult to test the API at the moment because the specification is so new and still in development. Only WebKit browsers support small bits of it. For this reason, this section does not contain any coding examples.

Similar to canvas, which you read about in Chapter 9, the Web Audio API contains a context for manipulating any audio data. It is this context that needs to be created to be able to use the API and is done via the AudioContext() constructor.

One of the main features of the API is the idea of modular routing, which allows arbitrary connections between different AudioNode objects—the building blocks of an AudioContext object. Each AudioNode can have inputs and/or outputs, which could be a stream of generated audio data or an audio file. As mentioned earlier, an AudioNode can connect to any other AudioNode, and you can call different methods on the different nodes to process the data within them in different ways through various interfaces. Through these interfaces, you can change the volumes of AudioNodes, attach them to audio or video elements, apply filters to them, apply linear affects to them, and/or spatialise them. In fact, processing is done through AudioNodes and processing is done to AudioNodes.

There's no denying that the Web Audio API will be a useful companion to the HTML5 Media API. Hopefully, the discussions of the W3C Audio Working Group will result in taking the best features of Mozilla's Audio Data API and the Web Audio API, and creating an even more powerful audio API. It's probably the first time that the word synergy comes to mind in the right context!

Let's move from audio to video and look at how video conferencing and similar functionality might be facilitated, beginning with the getUserMedia API.

When the HTML5 specification first came out, a number of features were identified as "post-HTML5," meaning that they were additions that should be kept in mind for the next generation of development.

One of these features was the ability to access external devices on a computer or phone (tablets weren't really in mainstream use at the time, although they're definitely relevant now!), such as a webcam or microphone. The initial idea put forward was to have an HTML device element that could be used, probably with the aid of an API, to access a device and allow for the taking of pictures and web conferencing.

This all changed in March 2011 when the device element was eliminated, and a new API was put forward—the getUserMedia API—to enable access to such devices.

> **NOTE:** You can view the current getUserMedia API at the WHATWG: www.whatwg.org/specs/web-apps/current-work/multipage/video-conferencing -and-peer-to-peer-communication.html#obtaining-local-multimedia-content.

The getUserMedia API is still very much in development, so there's actually little to show at this time. Back in March 2011, Opera implemented a test of this new API, but a special build of Opera Mobile for Android is required for the test (http://my.opera.com/core/blog/2011/03/23/webcam-orientation-preview).

When a specific device—for example, a webcam—is required to carry out a certain task, the user must be explicitly asked to allow the device to be accessed (the browser will implement this and use something like a pop-up window with yes/no buttons).

The API currently contains one method—getUserMedia—which accepts the following parameters:

- options. A comma-separated list of space-separated string tokens, the first token of which must be either:

  - audio. The media needs to include audio data.

  - video. The media needs to include video data; this token can be followed by either "user" or "environment" to indicate the preferred cameras to use. The specification is currently unclear as to what the difference between the two cameras might be.

- successCallback. This parameter specifies the function that is to be called with a parameter of type LocalMediaStream (you'll read about this in the section "Stream API" later in this chapter) if the user accepts the request to start using the required device.

- errorCallback. This parameter is optional and indicates the function to call when the user declines the request.

An example of getUserMedia being used to obtain access to a user's microphone might look like this:

```
navigator.getUserMedia('audio', audioReceived);
function audioReceived(stream) {
    // do stuff with the audio
}
```

The function audioReceived is set to be called on successCallback, which occurs when access to the microphone has been granted.

And an example of requesting access to a user's microphone and webcam for video conferencing might look like this:

```
navigator.getUserMedia('audio, video user', audioAndVideoReceived);
function audioAndVideoReceived(stream) {
    // do stuff with the audio and video
}
```

In this case, the audioAndVideoReceived function has been set to be called on successCallback.

Of course, these examples are based on the current recommendation, which is still under development and is likely to change in the future. But they give you an idea of how you might use the API. Such an API will be useful for implementing not only video conferencing, but also audio and webcam recordings, and live webcam streaming for use on the web.

Before you learn how to use the data from the local device, let's take a quick look at another proposed API, the PeerConnection API.

PEERCONNECTION API

The PeerConnection API allows connections to be made between different peers (e.g., web browsers), which in turn allow audio, video, and other data to be sent between the connected peers. Any connection between peers requires a communication, or signaling, channel, that is used to send messages between the peers and takes the form of XMLHttpRequest-based or WebSocket-based (you'll read more about WebSockets later in this chapter) communication.

A PeerConnection object is then created to which the addStream() method can be called to add any required audio and/or video streams to the connection. The addStream() method takes a parameter of type MediaStream, which represents a stream of media data, such as audio and video content from a webcam, which could be created as a result of a call to a getUserMedia() call of the getUserMedia API.

Again, the specification isn't complete and has yet to be implemented, but you can read about it at www.whatwg.org/specs/web-apps/current-work/multipage/video-conferencing-and-peer-to-peer-communication.html#peer-to-peer-connections.

Now you have two potential methods of obtaining a MediaStream object that contains audio and/or video data. But what can you actually do with these MediaStream objects? This is where the proposed Stream API comes in.

STREAM API

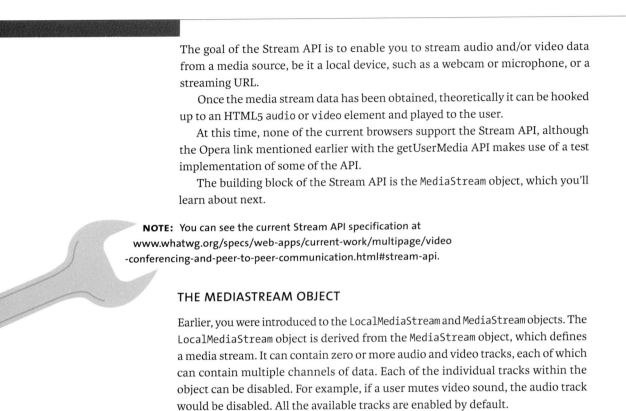

The goal of the Stream API is to enable you to stream audio and/or video data from a media source, be it a local device, such as a webcam or microphone, or a streaming URL.

Once the media stream data has been obtained, theoretically it can be hooked up to an HTML5 audio or video element and played to the user.

At this time, none of the current browsers support the Stream API, although the Opera link mentioned earlier with the getUserMedia API makes use of a test implementation of some of the API.

The building block of the Stream API is the MediaStream object, which you'll learn about next.

NOTE: You can see the current Stream API specification at
www.whatwg.org/specs/web-apps/current-work/multipage/video
-conferencing-and-peer-to-peer-communication.html#stream-api.

THE MEDIASTREAM OBJECT

Earlier, you were introduced to the LocalMediaStream and MediaStream objects. The LocalMediaStream object is derived from the MediaStream object, which defines a media stream. It can contain zero or more audio and video tracks, each of which can contain multiple channels of data. Each of the individual tracks within the object can be disabled. For example, if a user mutes video sound, the audio track would be disabled. All the available tracks are enabled by default.

A MediaStream object has an input and an output. If a MediaStream object is created as a result of a call to a getUserMedia() call of the getUserMedia API, the input will be the local device, such as a webcam or a microphone. If the MediaStream object is created as a result of a call to the PeerConnection API, the input will be the data received from the remote peer.

The MediaStream object also has a method called record(), which is used to start the attached device recording. In addition, the LocalMediaStream object has a stop() method, which stops the local device from streaming and/or recording.

The following example shows how the getUserMedia API and the Stream API might be used together to stream a webcam directly to an HTML5 video element:

```
<video autoplay></video>
<script>
    navigator.getUserMedia('video user', webcamReceived);
    function webcamReceived(webcamStream) {
        video.src = webcamStream;
    }
</script>
```

In the preceding code, the call to getUserMedia() returns a MediaStream object, which has been assigned the (arbitrary) variable name webcamStream and is then assigned to the video element's src parameter. Of course, this shows you how a simple example might work; there is currently no ability to test it on any of the major browsers.

Once again, the Stream API looks very promising toward delivering easy-to-build solutions for audio and webcam streaming, audio and video recording, and video conferencing. So the Stream API can help you stream data from these devices, but you first need to set up a connection, possibly using one of the APIs mentioned in the previous section. And you'll recall that WebSockets was mentioned earlier as a possible connection method for the PeerConnection API. Therefore, you'll look at WebSockets next.

WEBSOCKET API

WebSockets provide a method of setting up bidirectional communication between a browser and a server, which is "always-open" and runs directly on TCP rather than using HTTP. Previous HTTP methods used "long-polling," where the browser would constantly poll the server in an effort to ensure that the connection stays open.

Strictly speaking, the WebSocket API isn't a "future feature." You can actually use WebSockets now, even though they have yet to be fully standardised. Browser support varies: Safari has supported it since version 5, Chrome since version 10, and Opera has partially supported it since version 11. Firefox has supported a proprietary version since Firefox 4 (prefixed with "Moz").

Note: WebSockets are not actually part of HTML5. They have their own W3C specification at http://dev.w3.org/html5/websockets.

TIP: WebSockets are disabled by default in Opera 11.50, but you can enable them by typing about:config in the address bar and searching for "WebSockets."

The connection between the browser and the server is kept open; therefore, only the data that needs to be sent is actually sent, without any overheads. Compare this to Ajax calls, which set up a new HTTP request and exchange with every piece of data that needs to be sent.

NOTE: An overhead in this case is extra information in addition to the actual data to be sent that HTTP needs to send and receive with each request in order to communicate.

THE WEBSOCKET INTERFACE

The WebSocket interface is really quite simple to use. A WebSocket constructor (MozWebSocket in the case of Firefox) can accept two parameters: the url that specifies the URL of the WebSocket server to connect to and an optional protocols parameter, which is either a string or an array of strings that specifies the required protocol.

Once a connection has been made and a `WebSocket` object is returned, you can use a number of methods and attributes. **Tables 11.1** and **11.2** list these methods and attributes.

> **NOTE:** The specification isn't clear as to what string values the `WebSocket()` protocols **attribute can contain:**
>
> ```
> var con = new WebSocket('wss://echo.websocket.org');
> ```
>
> This code attempts to obtain a connection to the wss://echo.websocket.org WebSocket server.

TABLE 11.1 WebSocket Methods

METHOD	DESCRIPTION
send(data)	Sends the specified data across the open connection. The data can be a string, an ArrayBuffer, or a Blob.
close()	Closes the open connection.

TABLE 11.2 WebSocket Attributes

ATTRIBUTE	DESCRIPTION
readyState	Contains the current state of the WebSocket connection, which can be one of the following (corresponding integer values are shown in brackets): • CONNECTING (0). The connection has not yet been established. • OPEN (1). The connection is established and communication across it is possible. • CLOSING (2). The connection is currently closing down. • CLOSED (3). The connection has been closed or could not be opened.
bufferedAmount	Contains the number of bytes that have been queued up using the send() method but have not yet been sent across the connection. This does not include any overheads used by the protocol.
extensions	Contains the extensions selected by the server (if any).
protocols	Contains the subprotocol that the server has selected for use (if any).

When the WebSocket connection is open, you can use the `send()` method to send any data across the connection to the WebSocket server. Of course, you need to know when the WebSocket connection is open before you can do that. For that, of course, you need to wait for events. Four such events are specified by the specification, and they're listed in **Table 11.3**.

TABLE 11.3 WebSocket Events

EVENT	DESCRIPTION
onopen	Raised when a WebSocket connection has been successfully made to the server in question.
onmessage	Raised when a message has been received over the open WebSocket connection.
onclose	Raised when the open WebSocket connection is closed.
onerror	Raised when the open WebSocket connection reports an error.

And that's it for the WebSocket interface. The next section will put some of these methods, attributes, and events together using a simple example.

USING WEBSOCKETS

Using what you've just read about in the preceding section, let's construct a simple WebSocket example that opens a WebSocket connection and sends and receives data from a WebSocket server.

NOTE: Setting up a WebSocket server is outside the scope of this book, but you can set up your own using node.js. Remy Sharp details an account of how you might do this at http://remysharp.com/slicehost-nodejs-websockets.

For this example, you'll use the wss://echo.websocket.org WebSocket server, which is freely available and simply echoes back the data that you send to it.

You first need to set up some HTML that allows the connection to be opened and closed, and data sent via some simple buttons. You also need an input field to enter the message to send and then a simple div to display the data that was sent and received:

```
<div>
    Connection Status: <span id="conStatus">Closed</span>
</div>
<button id="connect" onclick="connect()">connect</button>
<button id="close" onclick="closeConnection()">close</button>
<div>
    <label for="msg">Message</label>
    <input id="msg" type="text" />
    <button id="send" onclick="send()">send</button>
</div>
<div id="display"></div>
```

Let's walk through the required JavaScript code.

You first need to define a variable to store the WebSocket connection:

```
var con;
```

Now let's look at the connect() function:

```
function connect() {
    con = new WebSocket('wss://echo.websocket.org');
    con.onopen = function () {
        setStatus("Open");
    };
    con.onmessage = function (e) {
        displayMsg("Server: " + e.data);
    };
```

```
con.onclose = function (e) {
    setStatus("Closed");
};
con.onerror = function (error) {
    setStatus("Error " + error);
};
}
```

You start by making a call to the WebSocket constructor to open the connection. Then you assign different functions to each of the events mentioned in Table 11.3 to be called when that particular event is raised.

The setStatus() function simply changes the status message in the conStatus span defined in the HTML:

```
function setStatus(status) {
    document.getElementById('conStatus').innerHTML = status;
}
```

Similarly, the displayMsg() function simply appends the string in question to the display div:

```
function displayMsg(msg) {
    document.getElementById('display').innerHTML += msg + "<br />";
}
```

The closeConnection() function checks to see if the connection is closed (connection state 3), and if not, calls the close() method on the WebSocket object:

```
function closeConnection() {
    if (con.readyState != 3) con.close();
}
```

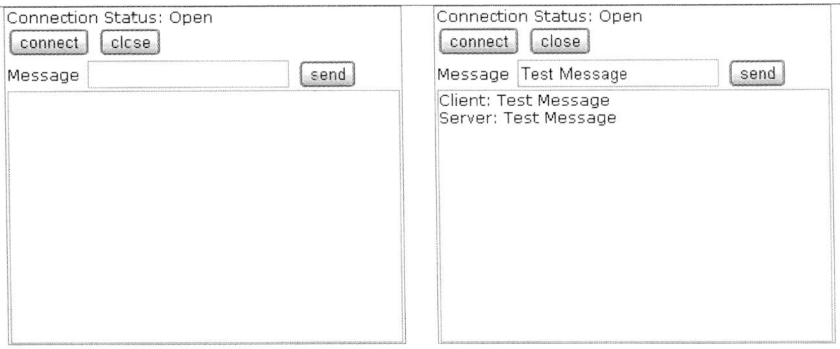

FIGURE 11.3 After clicking the Connect button and opening the connection (left), a test message is sent across the open WebSocket and echoed to the screen (right).

And last but by no means least, the send() function checks to see if the connection is actually open (connection state 1), reads the value entered in the msg input field, displays the value onscreen, and then sends it across the open connection:

```
function send() {
    if (con.readyState == 1) {
        var msg = document.getElementById("msg").value;
        displayMsg("Client: " + msg);
        con.send(msg);
    }
}
```

The resulting code is not much to look at, but it neatly shows how easy it is to use the WebSocket API for two-way communication with a WebSocket server.

Figure 11.3 shows how the preceding code might look in action.

NOTE: The code for this example is available at www.html5multimedia.com.

So what do WebSockets have to do with HTML5 media? Well, that's a good question, because in any related application, the Stream API will be used in the future to stream any audio and video data. But in an application that uses streaming audio and video, it's also quite possible that other data might need to be transferred. For example, as mentioned earlier, the PeerConnection API might utilise WebSockets for communication between peers. In addition, imagine that you have a video chat application that you also want to add text chat to (in case users want to mute the sound).

At the moment, there are, of course, a number of applications available that provide functionality such as video and audio chat, but they're just that, applications. They need to be installed.

Similarly through the browser, you can also use Flash to provide the same functionality, but again that requires something extra to be installed, in this case a third-party plugin. And recall that the iPad, for example, doesn't support Flash.

In the future, having all this capability built in to the browser means that as long as the browser supports these APIs (which all major browsers should, eventually), nothing more will be needed to deliver the required functionality. It will just work. And that is indeed a step in the right direction.

WRAPPING **UP**

The future features you've learned about in this chapter have given you an idea of what you might need to be learning more about if you're thinking about implementing more than audio and video on your website.

The proposed Audio API, once it's finished, will allow you to manipulate audio before playing it to your users, for say, taking advantage of an advanced sound setup. Game developers will also benefit from the extended API because it will allow them to dynamically create and edit sound.

Creating simple video conferencing is a step closer to reality with the upcoming getUserMedia, PeerConnection, and Stream APIs. These should work well together to help you deliver a streaming video and audio solution to your users.

And finally, the WebSocket API allows you to enhance your websites and applications that use the other APIs discussed in this chapter, allowing data to be transferred efficiently across web connections.

This final chapter supports the fact that HTML5 multimedia is still undergoing change and growing. And even though the specification is currently in "Last Call" (for changes), other specifications that will help enhance HTML5 will continue to grow from it.

Never stop learning, because you can never know enough or everything.

INDEX

F

fast forward button, adding, 110–111
feColorMatrix filter, 233
feGaussianBlur filter, applying, 236
figcaption element, 19
figure element, 19
fill attribute, setting to freeze, 231
fillRect() function, using with canvas,
    199–202
filter element definition, 233–237
Firefox
    audio support, 49
    video support, 64
Flash fallback, using with video files, 73
Flash file playback, providing, 55
Flash Player, 25–26, 29
    in Internet Explorer 8, 57–58
    using embed element, 56
Flash Player 10.2
    lack of support for, 27
    vulnerability in, 27
footer element, 10–11
Fraunhofer patent, 47
functions in JavaScript API
    addEventListener(), 102
    addTextTrack(), 97
    canPlayType(), 97
    changePlaybackSpeed(), 110
    changeVolume(), 105
    clearInterval() function, 206
    createElement(), 208
    drawImage(), 201
    fillRect(), 201–202
    findPos(), 113
    getImageData(), 209
    load(), 97
    Math.floor(), 105
    pause(), 97, 101

play(), 96–97, 101
playVideo(), 96
putImageData(), 209
setInterval() function, 205
setPlayPosition(), 112–113
toggleMute(), 106
togglePlay(), 101, 103
using, 96

G

Gasston, Peter, 80
Gaussian blur, applying to video, 236
German subtitles, specifying, 186
getImageData() function, using, 209
getUserMedia API, 247–248
    audio parameter, 247
    errorCallback parameter, 248
    microphone access, 248
    options parameter, 247
    successCallback parameter, 248
    video parameter, 247
Google Chrome
    enabling Web Audio API in, Web
        Audio API, 246
    opacity consideration, 146
    playbackRate attribute, 111
    video support, 64
gradients
    using in CSS3, 123–125
    using with video, 123–125
greyscale video, playing, 208–212

H

h element, using in header, 16
H.264 (MP4) video format, 63
Handbrake video encoder,
    downloading, 66

N

native multimedia
   audio element, 32, 52
   benefits, 31
   in Internet Explorer 9, 42
   in Safari, 42
   source element, 38–39
   track element, 40–41
   video element, 35–37
nav element, 10, 17
node.js website, 254

O

object element, using with plugins, 28–29
Ogg Vorbis audio format, 46, 49
   browser support for, 49
   using, 52
opacity value
   fading, 146–147
   using in CSS3, 122
Opera video support, 64, 133
Outlining Algorithm, 16

P

param element, using with plugins, 30
path element, using with SVG video
      masks, 231
PeerConnection API, 249
perspective property, using with 3D
      Transforms, 154
Pfeiffer, Silvia, 184
pixelData object, manipulating data in,
      210–211
pixels, setting transparency for, 235
playing video, copying, 205–207. See also
      video copy

Play/Pause button, adding, 98–102
Playr JavaScript library, 188–191
plugins. See also media players
   applet element, 28
   embed element, 28
   object element, 28
   param element, 30
   using with media players, 27
   wmode element, 30
print media type, 76
progress bar
   adding, 107–109
   adding for accessibility, 194
   updateProgress() function, 108–109
   using range element as, 193
projection media type, 76
ProtoFluid application, downloading, 79
putImageData() function, using, 209

Q

QuickTime multimedia player, 26
quirks mode, 9

R

range element, using as progress bar, 193
rastar graphics, 216
RealAudio player, 24
reflection, specifying on HTML elements,
      135–136
rewind button, adding, 110–111
RGB channels, converting, 235
right angle bracket (>), including in video
      cues, 183
rotate transform, using, 150, 164
rotate3d() transform, using, 167–168
rounded corners, using in CSS3, 126–127

S

Safari
  audio support, 49
  native multimedia in, 42
  playbackRate attribute, 111
  video support, 64
Scalable Vector Graphics (SVG)
  advantages, 216–217, 222
  browser support, 217
  circle element, 219
  ellipse element, 220
  fill attribute for text colour, 218
  text element, 218
scale transform, using, 148–150
screen media type, 76
screen shot
  drawImage() function, 202–203
  fillRect() function, 201–202
  loadedmetadata API event, 202
  ratio variable, 202
  snap() function, 203
  taking of HTML5 video, 201–204
script element, 20
section element, 13–16
seek bar, adding, 112–113
shadows, using in CSS3, 126–128
Sharp, Remy, 20, 254
Shockwave, 25
Sintel video cover animation, 162
sites
  2D API, 199
  2D Transforms, 153
  3D Transforms, 154, 157
  Android video support, 80
  animate element, 229
  animateMotion element, 231
  animation-play-state property, 160
  Audio Data API, 244

sites *(continued)*
  Blender Foundation, 162
  Camen Design, 75
  canvas basics, 200, 212
  Captionator JavaScript library, 188
  CSS2, 75
  CSS3 linear gradients, 125
  CSS3 specification, 122
  CSS3 Transitions specification, 147
  drawImage() function, 202
  Durian Open Movie Project, 162
  getUserMedia API, 247
  Handbrake, 66
  HTML5 Document Outlines, 16
  html5shim script, 20
  innerShiv script, 20
  JavaScript tutorial, 86
  js_videosub, 188
  jscaptions, 188
  JW Player, 55
  Kaltura, 188
  LeanBack Player JavaScript library, 188
  "Links and Anchors," 5
  mask property, 137
  Media Converter, 50, 66
  media queries, 76
  MediaElementJS JavaScript library, 188
  Miro Video Converter, 50, 66
  Modernizr detection library, 115
  MPEG (Moving Picture Experts Group), 63
  node.js, 254
  object-fit property, 134
  object-position property, 134
  PeerConnection API, 249
  Playr JavaScript library, 188
  ProtoFluid application, 79
  reflect property, 137
  Sintel video cover animation, 162
  Stream API, 250

WATCH
READ
CREATE

Unlimited online access to all Peachpit, Adobe Press, Apple Training and New Riders videos and books, as well as content from other leading publishers including: O'Reilly Media, Focal Press, Sams, Que, Total Training, John Wiley & Sons, Course Technology PTR, Class on Demand, VTC and more.

No time commitment or contract required! Sign up for one month or a year. **All for $19.99 a month**

SIGN UP TODAY
peachpit.com/creativeedge

creative
edge

05536212